D0876696

The Survival Papers

Marie-Louise von Franz, Honorary Patron

**Studies in Jungian Psychology
by Jungian Analysts**

Daryl Sharp, General Editor

The Survival Papers

Anatomy of a Midlife Crisis

DARYL SHARP

To Dave, Ben and Tanya

Canadian Cataloguing in Publication Data

Sharp, Daryl, 1936-
    The survival papers: anatomy of a midlife crisis

(Studies in Jungian psychology by Jungian analysts; 35)

Includes bibliographical references and index.

ISBN 0-919123-34-1

1. Middle age—Psychological aspects—Case Studies.
2. Life change events—Case studies. 3. Jung, C.G.
(Carl Gustav), 1875-1961. 4. Psychoanalysis.
5. Sharp, Daryl, 1936- . I. Title. II. Series.
BF724.6.S48 1988   155.6   C88-094042-5

Copyright © 1988 by Daryl Sharp.
All rights reserved.

INNER CITY BOOKS
Box 1271, Station Q, Toronto, Canada M4T 2P4
Telephone (416) 927-0355

Honorary Patron: Marie-Louise von Franz.
Publisher and General Editor: Daryl Sharp.
Senior Editor: Vicki Cowan.
Editorial Board: Fraser Boa, Daryl Sharp, Marion Woodman.
Production: David Sharp.

INNER CITY BOOKS was founded in 1980 to promote the
understanding and practical application of the work of C.G. Jung.

Cover: Portrait 1938, by Joan Miro (Kunsthaus, Zurich).

Index by Daryl Sharp.

Printed and bound in Canada by Webcom Limited

CONTENTS

Preface   9

Introduction   11
    Neurosis, Midlife Crisis and Individuation   11
    The Purpose of a Midlife Crisis   16
    Jung's Energic Viewpoint   19
    Adaptation and Breakdown   23
    The Self-Regulation of the Psyche   29

1   Difficulty at the Beginning   31

2   The Serpent Wakes   45

3   The Unknown Other   61

4   The Hero's Journey   77

5   Reality As We Know It   93

6   Toujours Grimace   105

7   The Middle of Nowhere   123

8   The Transcendent Function   127

9   The End of the Beginning   145

Epilogue   149

Index   152

See final pages for descriptions of other Inner City Books

Only what is really oneself has the power to heal.
—C.G. Jung, *Two Essays.*

Preface

A midlife crisis, like an acute neurosis, is characterized by conflict, depression and anxiety.

Contrary to the popular belief that such symptoms are unproductive indications of illness, C.G. Jung's view was that they are attempts at self-cure—manifestations of a basically healthy psyche trying to find a proper balance.

"The moment of the outbreak of neurosis is not just a matter of chance," writes Jung. "As a rule it is most critical. It is usually the moment when a new psychological adjustment, that is, a new adaptation, is demanded."[1]

In this light, a breakdown of the personality has a purpose: to force a person onto a new level of awareness.

This book draws on the basic concepts of Jungian psychology to explore the experience and meaning of conflict, depression and many other symptoms associated with psychological problems in the middle years of life.

---

[1] "Psychoanalysis and Neurosis," *Freud and Psychoanalysis,* CW 4, par. 563. [CW refers throughout to *The Collected Works of C.G. Jung* (Bollingen Series XX), 20 vols., trans. R.F.C. Hull, ed. H. Read, M. Fordham, G. Adler, Wm. McGuire; Princeton: Princeton University Press, 1953-1979.]

Introduction

The man with a neurosis who knows that he is neurotic is more individuated than the man without this consciousness. The man who is a damned nuisance to his surroundings and knows it is more individuated than the man who is blissfully unconscious of his nature.

—C.G. Jung, *Letters.*

Neurosis, Midlife Crisis and Individuation

The juxtaposition of neurosis, usually thought of as an illness, and individuation, a common term for healthy psychological development, may seem incongruous. And indeed, at first sight they are strange bedfellows.

However, in the school of thought that is called Jungian, a case may be made for neurosis as a prerequisite for the individuation process. The reason for this will become clear in the course of this book. Here it is enough to point out Jung's thumbnail description of neurosis as *disunity with oneself,* and individuation as *the conscious movement toward psychological wholeness.*

From this point of view, neurosis actually provides the impetus and the motivation for psychological development. Indeed, if one believes in the value of becoming conscious, then those "afflicted" with neurosis are in fact the lucky ones. A nervous breakdown is often a necessary prelude to a more meaningful and satisfying way of life. There are many people out there who know this to be true, and I am one of them.

A reporter for a local newspaper once came to interview me for a story about the different approaches to therapy. He didn't know much about Jungian psychology, he said apologetically. He consulted his notes. "Aren't you the people who believe in the disintegration of the personality?"

11

I had never thought about it quite like that, but when I looked into it I found that Jung had:

> A dissociation is not healed by being split off, but by more complete disintegration. All the powers that strive for unity, all healthy desire for selfhood, will resist the disintegration, and in this way he will become conscious of the possibility of an inner integration, which before he had always sought outside himself. He will then find his reward in an undivided self.
>
> This is what happens very frequently about the midday of life, and in this wise our miraculous human nature enforces the transition that leads from the first half of life to the second.[1]

The reporter's question reminded me of a time when I refused to believe in Detroit. In my mind it stood for material values and a way of life that I could not accept. And so I turned my back on Detroit and pretended it did not exist. In spite of me, however, cars continued to roll off the assembly line.

Many things happen whether we believe in them or not. It is a fact that personalities do break down. Overflowing consulting rooms are ample evidence of that. The real question is not whether but why, and to what purpose, if any.

The disintegration of the personality sounds much less ominous if it is understood as an opportunity for new life rather than the end of the line. Such an attitude is more than mere consolation for the person going through the experience; it can mean the difference between life and death, for it offers the possibility of meaning in what would otherwise be pointless suffering. This is especially true in the middle years of life, when many men and women are brought to their knees by the experience of their own psychology.

This book is not concerned with the differential diagnosis of neurotic conditions, nor with so-called narcissistic personality disorders. It is solely concerned with the psychological factors at work in an acute outbreak of neurosis, which for all practical purposes is indis-

---

[1] "Marriage as a Psychological Relationship," *The Development of Personality,* CW 17, pars. 334f.

tinguishable from a midlife crisis. This is in accordance with Jung's advice to psychotherapists:

> Diagnosis is a highly irrelevant affair since, apart from affixing a more or less lucky label to a neurotic condition, nothing is gained by it, least of all as regards prognosis and therapy. . . . It is enough to diagnose a "psychoneurosis" as distinct from some organic disturbance.[2]

A midlife crisis is marked by the sudden appearance of atypical moods and behavior patterns. Similar symptoms may occur in adolescents and young adults on the brink of life, and indeed in much older people, but their psychology is not the particular focus of this book.

This book is written for those in their middle years, male and female in more or less equal numbers, who have always managed quite well, have held down a job, perhaps married and had children, and then one day find that nothing works any more.

They suffer terrible moods that gnaw at their innards. They have dark thoughts, suspicions and fantasies that give them no peace. Their outlook is bleak. They lose their energy and ambition, they are anxious and feel they've missed the boat. They may ascribe their moods to the loss of a loved one, an unsatisfactory relationship, problems at work or any number of other objectively difficult circumstances. There is an inability to adapt to change, they cannot meet new or unexpected situations in their usual way. Sometimes there is a strong conscious conflict, but often there is nothing they can put a finger on. Where before they could cope with the vicissitudes of life, now they cannot. Life has no meaning. They hurt and they have thoughts of suicide.

In Jungian analysis, relatively little attention is paid to symptoms that to others might appear to be the main problem: anxiety, conflict, depression, fear, guilt, sleeplessness, etc. and etc. Time will take care of these. The real problem is the person who is experiencing

---

[2] "Medicine and Psychotherapy," *The Practice of Psychotherapy*, CW 16, par. 195.

them. Thus the aim of analysis is to bring to light the psychology of the individual.

How this is accomplished is different in every case. But the transformation of neurotic suffering into a new and healthier perspective on life—if indeed this happens, for analysis is not a panacea—has in every case more to do with motivation and innate potential than with anything the analyst says or does.

The most noticeable, and potentially valuable, symptom in a midlife crisis is conflict. "The apparently unendurable conflict," writes Jung, "is proof of the rightness of your life. A life without inner contradiction is either only half a life or else a life in the Beyond, which is destined only for angels."[3]

The more intense the conflict, the more pressing is the need to reestablish a vital connection between consciousness and the unconscious. The struggle to effect this is the path of individuation.

Individuation is a process informed by the archetypal ideal of wholeness. If we could always know what is "right" for us, our "true" direction, then we would live in complete inner harmony, always at peace, in Tao. This is the goal, essentially unattainable, whose very desirability often blinds one to the value and necessity of the process leading up to it.

As Jung puts it, "The goal is important only as an idea: the essential thing is the *opus* [the work on oneself] which leads to the goal: *that* is the goal of a lifetime."[4]

In other words, the aim of the individuation process is not to overcome one's personal psychology—to become perfect—but to become familiar with it.

Many men and women have been dragged kicking and screaming onto the path of individuation, envious of so-called normal people who appear to have no problems. This is to mistake unconsciousness

---

[3] *C.G. Jung Letters,* vol. 1 (Bollingen Series XCV:1), Princeton: Princeton University Press, 1973, p. 375.

[4] "The Psychology of the Transference," *The Practice of Psychotherapy,* CW 16, par. 400.

for wholeness. Wholeness, or at least the degree to which this is humanly possible, is only achieved through self-examination, and unless there are acknowledged problems there is nothing to examine.

Those who have a midlife crisis are caught in the grip of an inner necessity—a psychological imperative to embark on the journey of self-discovery. We cannot lightly escape this obligation. Jung refers to Goethe's *Faust,* where Mephisto mocks Faust for an impulse to withdraw to a "simple life":

> Right. There is one way that needs
> No money, no physician, and no witch.
> Pack up your things and get back to the land
> And there begin to dig and ditch;
> Keep to the narrow round, confine your mind,
> And live on fodder of the simplest kind,
> A beast among the beasts; and don't forget
> To use your own dung on the crops you set![5]

Jung adds his own comment: "There is of course nothing to stop [a man] from taking a two-room cottage in the country, or from pottering about in a garden and eating raw turnips. But his soul laughs at the deception."[6]

The simple life is an option only for those tied to it by outer necessity. The rest of us really have only two choices: to be a willing and conscious participant in our own individuation process or a hapless victim.

"This is as much as to say," writes Jung, "that anyone who is destined to descend into a deep pit had better set about it with all the necessary precautions rather than risk falling into the hole backwards."[7]

---

[5] *Two Essays on Analytical Psychology,* CW 7, par. 258.
[6] Ibid.
[7] *Aion,* CW 9ii, par. 125.

The Purpose of a Midlife Crisis

In the American Heritage Dictionary there is the following definition of neurosis:

> Any of various functional disorders of the mind or emotions, without obvious organic lesion or change, and involving anxiety, phobia, or other abnormal behavior symptoms. Also called "psychoneurosis."

That does not sound promising, and certainly carries no hint that it might be valuable or have a purpose. It simply reflects the general view of neurosis as a sickness, as something unhealthy, "abnormal." It is a natural extension of the medical model of physical illness, according to which diseases are a pathological abberation; they exist only to be cured.

In terms of this causal model, psychological symptoms have the same function as, say, a headache. They tell you the nature of an underlying disease which can then be eradicated. Thus we blithely pop tranquilizers to banish depression.

Jung's view, on the other hand, is that an outbreak of neurosis is an opportunity to become conscious, that is, to wake up to who we are as opposed to who we think we are. Through neurosis and the symptoms that accompany it, we come face to face with our limitations—but we may also discover our strengths and our true nature. From this standpoint neurosis is like an alarm clock, and takes on a rather more positive role than the medical community and most laymen are inclined to ascribe to it.

In 1935 Jung gave a series of talks to a group of doctors in London. In a question period there is the following exchange:

Question: "Would Professor Jung give us a definition of neurosis?"

Jung: "A neurosis is a dissociation of personality due to the existence of complexes. To have complexes is in itself normal; but if the complexes are incompatible, that part of the personality which is too contrary to the conscious part becomes split off. . . .

"As the split-off complexes are unconscious, they find only an indirect means of expression, that is, through neurotic symptoms. . . .

Any incompatibility of character can cause dissociation, and too great a split between the thinking and the feeling function, for instance, is already a slight neurosis. When you are not quite at one with yourself in a given matter, you are approaching a neurotic condition." . . .

Question: "I think we can assume, then, Professor Jung, that you regard the outbreak of a neurosis as an attempt at self-cure, as an attempt at compensation in bringing out the inferior function?"

Jung: "Absolutely."

Question: "I understand, then, that the outbreak of a neurotic illness, from the point of view of a person's development, is something favorable?"

Jung: "That is so, and I am glad you bring up that idea. That is really my point of view. . . . In many cases we have to say, 'Thank heaven he could make up his mind to be neurotic.' Neurosis is really an attempt at self-cure, just as any physical illness is partly an attempt at self-cure. . . . It is an attempt of the self-regulating psychic system to restore the balance, in no way different from the function of dreams—only rather more forceful and drastic."[8]

Jung's belief is that in a psychological crisis unconscious contents are automatically activated in an attempt to compensate the one-sided attitude of consciousness. This is true at any age, but it is not usually necessary in the first half of life to deal with what Jung calls the problem of opposites—the disparity between conscious ego attitudes and what is going on in the unconscious.[9]

The problems of young people, notes Jung, "generally come from a collision between the forces of reality and an inadequate, infantile attitude, which from the causal point of view is characterized by an abnormal dependence on the real or imaginary parents."[10] Therapy in these cases usually involves transferring the imagos of the parents

---

8 "The Tavistock Lectures," *The Symbolic Life,* CW 18, pars. 382ff.

9 "There is no form of human tragedy," writes Jung, "that does not in some measure proceed from this conflict between the ego and the unconscious." ("Analytical Psychology and 'Weltanschauung,' " *The Structure and Dynamics of the Psyche,* CW 8, par. 706)

10 *Two Essays,* CW 7, par. 88.

onto more suitable substitute figures, and encouraging the development of a strong ego.

But for those in middle life, "development no longer proceeds via the dissolution of infantile ties, the destruction of infantile illusions and the transference of old imagos to new figures: it proceeds via the problem of opposites."[11] Thus the ability to hold the tension that arises in an inner conflict is of paramount importance; indeed, this is only possible when a firm ego has already been established.

Jung's so-called synthetic or purposive view of neurosis is not necessarily incompatible with the traditional psychoanalytic reductive view, namely that psychological problems are primarily sexual in nature and stem from Oedipal conflicts in childhood. It is truer to say that the two views are complementary: Freud looks to the past for the cause of psychic discomfort in the present; Jung focuses on the present with an eye to what is possible in the future.

Jung did not dispute Freudian theory that Oedipal fixations can manifest as neurosis in later life. He agreed that certain periods in life, and particularly infancy, often have a permanent and determining influence on the personality. He simply pointed out that this was an insufficient explanation for those cases in which there was no trace of neurosis until the time of the breakdown.

> If the fixation were indeed real [i.e., the primary cause] we should expect to find its influence constant; in other words, a neurosis lasting throughout life. This is obviously not the case. The psychological determination of a neurosis is only partly due to an early infantile predisposition; it must be due to some cause in the present as well. And if we carefully examine the kind of infantile fantasies and occurrences to which the neurotic is attached, we shall be obliged to agree that there is nothing in them that is specifically neurotic. Normal individuals have pretty much the same inner and outer experiences, and may be attached to them to an astonishing degree without developing a neurosis.[12]

---

[11] Ibid., par. 91.

[12] "Psychoanalysis and Neurosis," *Freud and Psychoanalysis,* CW4, par. 564.

What, then, determines why one person has a midlife crisis while another, perhaps in equally difficult circumstances, does not? Jung's answer to this is that the individual psyche knows both its limits and its potential. If the former are being exceeded, or the latter not realized, a breakdown occurs. The psyche itself acts to correct the situation.

Jung's Energic Viewpoint

Together with the hypothesis of fixation, Freud proposed that the incestuous desires of the Oedipus complex were the primary cause of the neurotic's characteristic regression to infantile fantasies.

Although Jung accepted this view for some years, in 1913 he broke with Freud's Vienna school of psychoanalysis when he introduced an energic viewpoint into the psychology of neurosis:

> All psychological phenomena can be considered as manifestations of energy, in the same way that all physical phenomena have been understood as energic manifestations ever since Robert Mayer discovered the law of the conservation of energy. Subjectively and psychologically, this energy is conceived as *desire*. I call it *libido*, using the word in its original sense, which is by no means only sexual. . . .
>
> From a broader standpoint libido can be understood as vital energy in general, or as Bergson's *élan vital.*[13]

Psychic events, writes Jung, are analogous to physical events; both can be viewed from either a mechanistic or an energic standpoint:

> The mechanistic view is purely causal; it conceives an event as the effect of a cause, in the sense that unchanging substances change their relations to one another according to fixed laws. The energic point of view on the other hand is in essence final. . . . The flow of energy has a definite direction (goal) in that it follows the gradient of potential in a way that cannot be reversed.[14]

---

[13] Ibid., pars. 567f.

[14] "On Psychic Energy," *The Structure and Dynamics of the Psyche,* CW8, pars. 2f.

Jung felt that both views were valid, depending on the individual case. "Expediency, that is to say, the possibility of obtaining results, alone decides whether the one or the other view is to be preferred."[15]

With respect to neurosis—which both Jung and Freud saw in terms of a blockage of libido—the mechanistic or reductive view traces the problem back to a primary cause, while the energic or final view asks what is the intention of the psyche as a whole; where does the energy "want" to go?

As indicated above, Jung suggests there is a conservation of energy within the psyche, similar to that in the physical world. He refers to the principle of equivalence, a law in physics, which states that for a given quantity of energy expended or consumed in bringing about a certain condition, an equal amount of the same or another form of energy will appear elsewhere.

Psychologically, this means that where there is an overabundance of energy in one place, some other psychic function has been deprived; conversely, when libido "disappears," as it does in depression, it must appear in another form, for instance as a symptom.

> Every time we come across a person who has a "bee in his bonnet," or a morbid conviction, or some extreme attitude, we know that there is too much libido, and that the excess must have been taken from somewhere else where, consequently, there is too little. . . . Thus the symptoms of a neurosis must be regarded as exaggerated functions over-invested with libido.
>
> The question has to be reversed in the case of those syndromes characterized mainly by lack of libido, for instance apathetic states. Here we have to ask, where did the libido go? The libido is there, but it is not visible and is inaccessible to the patient himself. . . . It is the task of psychoanalysis to search out that hidden place where the libido dwells . . . . The hidden place is the "non-conscious," which we may also call the "unconscious" without attributing to it any mystical significance.[16]

---

15 Ibid., par. 6.
16 "The Theory of Psychoanalysis," *Freud and Psychoanalysis,* CW 4, pars. 254f.

While Jung acknowledged that reductive interpretations of neurosis can be valuable, he himself favored the energic or final viewpoint and considered it indispensable to any theory of psychological development. The causal view of regression, for instance, sees it determined by, say, a mother fixation. But from the final standpoint, writes Jung, "the libido regresses to the *imago* of the mother in order to find there the memory associations by means of which further development can take place."[17]

The difference between the personal mother and the "imago" of the mother is the difference between a complex and an archetypal image. Behind the complex—the accretion of emotional associations with one's personal mother—there is everything that has ever been associated with "mother," both positive and negative, in the history of mankind—the archetype of mother.

Regressed energy activates not only personal memories but archetypal images or symbols of, say, "mother," that may never have been personally experienced.

Jung stresses that "what to the causal view is *fact* to the final view is *symbol,* and vice versa. Everything that is real and essential to the one is unreal and inessential to the other."[18]

An exclusively causal view of neurosis, notes Jung, may actually inhibit development, since it binds the libido to the past and to elementary facts (for instance, a fixation to the personal mother). The final view, on the other hand, encourages development by transforming causes into means to an end, "into symbolic expressions for the way that lies ahead":

> Psychic development cannot be accomplished by intention and will alone; it needs the attraction of the symbol, whose value quantum [i.e, the energy invested in it] exceeds that of the cause. But the formation of a symbol cannot take place until the mind has dwelt long enough on the elementary facts, that is to say until the inner or outer

---

[17] "On Psychic Energy," *The Structure and Dynamics of the Psyche,* CW 8, par. 43.

[18] Ibid., par. 45.

necessities of the life-process have brought about a transformation of energy.[19]

The transformation of energy in this way is, as we shall see below, central to Jung's idea of what happens in neurosis. It involves both the principle of equivalence, mentioned above, and the principle of entropy, according to which the transformation of energy in a closed system is only possible as a result of differences in the intensity of energy that exists between different elements in that system.

Mix a glass of hot water with cold, for instance, and you end up with warm water. The transfer of energy from one to the other leads to an equalization of differences. Within the system there is a transformation.

Jung applied this principle to the psyche, with specific reference to what occurs in a conflict situation:

> Psychologically, we can see this process at work in the development of a lasting and relatively unchanging attitude. After violent oscillations at the beginning the opposites equalize one another, and gradually a new attitude develops, the final stability of which is the greater in proportion to the magnitude of the initial differences. The greater the tension between the pairs of opposites, the greater will be the energy that comes from them. . . .
>
> Daily psychological experience affords proof of this . . . . The most intense conflicts, if overcome, leave behind a sense of security and calm which is not easily disturbed, or else a brokenness that can hardly be healed. Conversely, it is just these intense conflicts and their conflagration which are needed in order to produce valuable and lasting results.[20]

Jung compared the flow of libido to a river: "The libido has, as it were, a natural penchant: it is like water, which must have a gradient if it is to flow."[21] This is an eminently practical consideration in a midlife crisis, where the flow of energy is blocked. The problem in each particular case is to find the appropriate gradient.

---

[19] Ibid., par. 47.
[20] Ibid., pars. 49f.
[21] *Symbols of Transformation,* CW 5, par. 337.

Here it is not a matter of will power, of rationally choosing an object or direction toward which the energy "ought" to flow. The question, again, is where does it naturally "want" to go? "What is it," asks Jung, "at this moment and in this individual, that represents the natural urge of life? That is the question."[22]

This regularly raises a moral dilemma and heightens an already existing conflict, which is precisely what is required. "There is no energy unless there is a tension of opposites," writes Jung. "Hence it is necessary to discover the opposite to the attitude of the conscious mind."[23] This involves bringing to light psychic contents that have been repressed.

> The repressed content must be made conscious so as to produce a tension of opposites, without which no forward movement is possible. The conscious mind is on top, the shadow underneath, and just as high always longs for low and hot for cold, so all consciousness, perhaps without being aware of it, seeks its unconscious opposite, lacking which it is doomed to stagnation, congestion, and ossification. Life is born only of the spark of opposites.[24]

Adaptation and Breakdown

The process of development from child to adult entails an increasing adaptation to the external world. Whenever a person's libido, in the process of adaptation, meets an obstacle, there is an accumulation of energy that normally gives rise to an increased effort to overcome the obstacle.

But if the obstacle seems to be insurmountable and the individual abandons the task of overcoming it, the stored-up energy regresses, that is, reverts to an earlier mode of adaptation. This in turn, writes Jung, activates infantile fantasies and wishes:

---

22 *Two Essays,* CW 7, par. 487.
23 Ibid., par. 78.
24 Ibid.

The best examples of such regressions are found in hysterical cases where a disappointment in love or marriage has precipitated a neurosis. There we find those well-known digestive disorders, loss of appetite, dyspeptic symptoms of all sorts, etc. . . . [typically accompanied by] a regressive revival of reminiscences from the distant past. We then find a reactivation of the parental imagos, of the Oedipus complex. Here the events of early infancy—never before important—suddenly become so. They have been regressively reactivated. Remove the obstacle from the path of life and this whole system of infantile fantasies at once breaks down and becomes as inactive and ineffective as before.[25]

For these reasons, Jung declared that he did not seek the cause of a neurosis in the past, but in the present: "I ask, what is the necessary task which the patient will not accomplish?"[26] In other words, in terms of the developmental process described above, "the psychological trouble in neurosis, and the neurosis itself, can be formulated as *an act of adaptation that has failed.*"[27]

As already indicated, this view of neurosis is quite different from the classical Freudian view, but it does not substantially change what happens in the process of analysis. The fantasies still have to be brought to light because the energy the person needs for health—that is, for adaptation—is attached to them. The object, however, is not to reveal a supposed root cause of the neurosis but to establish a connection between the conscious mind and the unconscious. Only in this way can the split-off energy become available for the accomplishment of the "necessary task" the person balks at.

"Considered from this standpoint," writes Jung, "psychoanalysis no longer appears as a mere reduction of the individual to his primitive sexual wishes, but, if rightly understood, as a highly moral task of immense educational value."[28]

---

[25] "Psychoanalysis and Neurosis," *Freud and Psychoanalysis,* CW4, par. 569.

[26] Ibid., par. 570.

[27] Ibid., par. 574.

[28] Ibid., par. 575.

Jung's view of neurosis as an attempt at self-cure—which in fact Freud shared to some extent—and his application of the conservation of energy theory to psychological phenomena are cornerstones in the practice of analytical psychology.

A basic assumption in the case of depression, for instance, is that the energy not available to consciousness has not simply vanished but is busily stirring up unconscious contents that for the sake of psychological health need to be brought to light and examined.

Thus, while a well-meaning friend might advise a depressed person to seek out a distraction—"Get out more, mix with other people, stop thinking about yourself"—the analyst sees the depression, or indeed any overwhelming mood, as a challenge to find out what is going on inside. Hence one is encouraged to introspect, to stay with the mood, to go into it rather than try to escape it.

In the normal course of life there is a relatively easy progression of libido, which is to say one's energy may be directed more or less at will. "Progression," writes Jung, "could be defined as the daily advance of the process of psychological adaptation."[29] This is not the same as development; progression refers simply to the continuous flow or current of life.

In order to satisfy the demands of adaptation it is necessary to adopt or attain an attitude appropriate to given circumstances. As long as circumstances do not change, there is no reason for one's attitude to change. But since circumstances do change, whether suddenly or over time, there is no one attitude that is permanently suitable.

Any change in the environment demands a new adaptation, which in turn requires a change in the attitude that was previously quite adequate. But a suitable attitude—that is, one that works in a given situation—is invariably characterized by a certain one-sidedness and is therefore resistant to change. When a particular attitude is no longer appropriate for the external situation, the stage is set for neurosis.

---

[29] "On Psychic Energy," *The Structure and Dynamics of the Psyche,* CW 8, par. 60.

For example, a feeling-attitude that seeks to fulfil the demands of reality by means of empathy may easily encounter a situation that can only be solved through thinking. In this case the feeling-attitude breaks down and the progression of libido ceases. The vital feeling that was present before disappears, and in its place the psychic value of certain conscious contents increases in an unpleasant way; subjective contents and reactions press to the fore and the situation becomes full of affect and ripe for explosions.[30]

Such symptoms indicate a damming up of libido, which is always marked by the breaking up of pairs of opposites.

During the progression of libido the pairs of opposites are united in the co-ordinated flow of psychic processes. . . . But in the stoppage of libido that occurs when progression has become impossible, positive and negative can no longer unite in co-ordinated action, because both have attained an equal value which keeps the scales balanced. . . . The tension leads to conflict, the conflict leads to attempts at mutual repression, and if one of the opposing forces is successfully repressed a dissociation ensues, a splitting of the personality, or disunion with oneself.[31]

The struggle between the opposites would continue unabated if the process of regression, the backward movement of libido, did not set in with the outbreak of the conflict.

Through their collision the opposites are gradually deprived of value and depotentiated. . . . In proportion to the decrease in value of the conscious opposites there is an increase in value of all those psychic processes which are not concerned with outward adaptation and therefore are seldom or never employed consciously.[32]

As the energic value of these previously unconscious psychic processes increases, they manifest indirectly as disturbances of conscious behavior, for example in what Freud described as symptomatic actions and in those emotional symptoms characteristic of neurosis.

---

[30] Ibid., par. 61.

[31] Ibid.

[32] Ibid., par. 62.

Jung's view is that since the stoppage of libido is due to a failure of the dominant conscious attitude, the unconscious contents activated by regression contain the seeds of a new progression. In terms of Jung's model of typology,[33] the unconscious contents include one's opposite attitude which, with the inferior functions, is potentially capable of complementing or even of replacing the inadequate conscious attitude.

> If thinking fails as the adapted function, because it is dealing with a situation to which one can adapt only by feeling, then the unconscious material activated by regression will contain the missing feeling function, although still in embryonic form, archaic and undeveloped. Similarly, in the opposite type, regression would activate a thinking function that would effectively compensate the inadequate feeling.[34]

The regression of energy thus confronts one with the problem of one's own psychology, as opposed to the initial difficulty of adapting to outer circumstances. In Jung's words, "regression leads to the necessity of adapting to the inner world of the psyche."[35]

Prominent aspects of the psyche that one needs to become aware of in such a situation are the persona (the "I" one presents to the outer world), the contrasexual complex (the inner feminine or anima in a man, the inner masculine or animus in a woman) and the shadow (all those things about oneself, both good and bad, that have either been repressed or never been conscious).

Looked at in this way, regression is not an abnormal symptom but as much a necessary phase in the developmental process as is progression.

It might seem from this description that the progression of energy —adaptation to outer conditions—is conceptually analogous to extraversion, and regression—requiring adaptation to inner condi-

---

[33] See below, chapter 5.

[34] "On Psychic Energy," *The Structure and Dynamics of the Psyche,* CW 8, par. 65.

[35] Ibid., par. 66.

tions—is comparable to introversion. According to Jung, this is not the case:

> Progression is a forwards movement of life in the same sense that time moves forwards. This movement can occur in two different forms: either extraverted, when the progression is predominantly influenced by objects and environmental conditions, or introverted, when it has to adapt itself to the conditions of the ego (or, more accurately, of the "subjective factor"). Similarly, regression can proceed along two lines: either as a retreat from the outside world (introversion), or as a flight into extravagant experience of the outside world (extraversion). Failure in the first case drives a man into a state of dull brooding, and in the second case into leading the life of a wastrel.[36]

It will now be apparent the extent to which Jung's view of neurosis as an attempt at self-cure is based on the belief that the psyche is a self-regulating system.

This accords with the general experience that in a conflict situation, for instance, advice and suggestion have no lasting effect.

"A real solution," writes Jung, "comes only from within, and then only because the patient has been brought to a different attitude."[37]

In practice, the conflict must be solved on a level of character where the opposites are taken sufficiently into account, "and this again is possible only through a change of character. . . . In such cases external solutions are worse than none at all."[38]

A summary of what happens psychologically in a midlife crisis appears on the opposite page. The following chapters will elaborate on the themes introduced here and show the self-regulating process at work in a particular individual.

---

[36] Ibid., par. 77.

[37] "Some Crucial Points in Psychoanalysis" (Jung-Loy Correspondence), *Freud and Psychoanalysis,* CW4, par. 606.

[38] Ibid., par. 607.

The Self-Regulation of the Psyche

1. Difficulty of adaptation. Difficulty of progression of energy.

2. Regression of libido (depression, lack of disposable energy).

3. Activation of unconscious contents (infantile fantasies, complexes, archetypal images, inferior function, opposite attitude, shadow, anima/animus, etc.). Compensation.

4. Formation of neurotic symptoms (confusion, fear, anxiety, guilt, moods, emotional reactions, etc.).

5. Unconscious or half-conscious conflict between ego and contents activated in the unconscious. Inner tension. Defensive reactions.

6. Activation of the transcendent function, involving the Self and archetypal patterns of wholeness.

7. Formation of symbols (numinosity, synchronicity).

8. Transfer of energy between unconscious contents and consciousness. Enlargement of the ego, more adequate progression of energy.

9. Integration of unconscious contents. The process of individuation.

1

Difficulty at the Beginning

When an inner situation is not made conscious,
it happens outside, as fate.
> —C.G. Jung, *Aion.*

Times of growth are beset with difficulties. They resemble a first
birth. But these difficulties arise from the very profusion of all
that is struggling to attain form. Everything is in motion: there-
fore if one perseveres there is a prospect of great success . . . .
Likewise, it is very important not to remain alone; in order to
overcome the chaos he needs helpers.
> —I Ching, Hexagram 3, "Difficulty at the Beginning."

Norman sat crying in my waiting room. I learned later that he had
been sitting there for close to an hour, waiting for his appointment.
My secretary had given him a cup of tea. His hands shook and he'd
spilled some on his pants.

I ushered him in and he collapsed into a leather wing-chair.

It was our first session together. He was not the strangest looking
person I'd seen in fifteen years as an analyst. But he wasn't the most
ordinary either. His hair was long; he had a beard and a moustache,
both neatly trimmed. He was perhaps in his late thirties, but he could
pass for ten years younger. He was cleanly dressed, a sport shirt under a light woolen sweater. The Hush Puppies seemed out of place.
His eyes were red and swollen.

"I'm sorry about this," he said, blowing his nose. "I started crying
when I got on the bus. I couldn't stop, I don't know why. I got here
early because I had nowhere else to go."

I said nothing.

"I'm very unhappy," he said. "I woke up crying a few days ago
and I've hardly stopped since. I'm glad you could see me at such

short notice. I don't know what to believe anymore. I'm so damned confused. Maybe I'm crazy. Sometimes I think I'd be better off dead. I don't know what to do."

He had a worn leather briefcase with him. He opened it and took out a notebook.

"I really have a wonderful life, a wife and two kids. They mean the world to me. I would die without them."

He started crying again. "I'm falling apart," he said.

"We've been happily married for six years. I love my wife, there is no possibility that I would leave her." He shrugged. "It's true I've been with other women, but they didn't mean anything to me. I couldn't live without my family." He look at me defiantly. "I did not come here because of them. The problem is mine. My kids are great. My wife is the best mother in the world. She loves me, she'd never leave me, I know that."

We sat for awhile in silence. I watched him. He was staring at the wall. I was sizing him up, assessing how I'd feel about working with this man. He was seeing phantoms of his own.

"I guess it all started about two years ago, when my wife told me she didn't like making love to me." He blew his nose.

"I had no idea," he said.

"Well, that's not quite true. I guess I knew she wasn't very interested after the first year or so. But it broke my heart to hear her say it. I was in Detroit at the time, closing a deal. I'd called from my hotel room to say hello to her and the kids. I like to keep in touch. There was a girl with me, I don't remember her name. My wife said, 'Please come home, we have to talk.' 'What about,' I said. 'About sex,' she said, 'it doesn't work between us.' She was crying, I was crying. I dropped everything and flew home right away."

Norman looked at his notebook. "Nothing's been the same since then. We talked about it, but there wasn't much to say. I stopped seeing other women—well, not counting that stewardess and the barmaid in Cincinnati—and read some books about technique. It didn't change anything. Oh, she wouldn't refuse me. Never had, never has. She's always been there for me. But she still doesn't enjoy it." He wiped his nose.

"I could live with that. It wasn't easy, but I could manage. We think alike, we do everything together. Sex isn't that important, I know that. We're the perfect couple, everyone envies us."

He looked at me with some pride.

"Then about a year ago she started seeing this other man. A great guy, he's an artist. Boris and his wife have been friends of ours for years. We play bridge together. I thought something was going on but she said no, it was just my imagination.

"Then I found some love letters—but I couldn't tell her because she'd be furious if she knew I'd been snooping in her things. Anyway, I believe she has a right to some fun. Sure I'm jealous, but that's my problem. I know he's no threat to our life together. I'd do anything to make things right."

Tears were running down his face. He left them there.

"I've been spying on them for months. I hide behind bushes, listen to their phone calls. I feel really ashamed of that but I can't help it. I always have this big knot in my stomach, wondering what they're up to. On top of her not wanting to make love to me I just can't stand the idea that she would with someone else. That's why I'm here. I should be able to accept that. I don't want to be so possessive. There's something wrong with me."

He brought out some pictures. "This is my wife Nancy, the kids —that's Ian, he's five and a half, and Jennifer, she's four—that's our house.

"I have a good job, but I haven't been able to work much lately. When I'm feeling bad I go into the basement and smoke some grass. I think about how things used to be, how happy we were. Sometimes it helps, sometimes I just feel worse."

"How did you find me?" I asked. "Why come to a Jungian?"

"A what?"

"A Jungian analyst."

Norman wiped his eyes. "You were recommended by a friend."

He looked at me with great sadness. "I'm depressed, I don't sleep well. I can't eat and I don't have any energy. So what do you think I should do?"

*

I did not know what Norman should do, but for selfish reasons I was glad to see him.

My life and practice had become routine. I could hardly remember the quiet desperation that took me into analysis twenty years ago. Norman was a timely reminder of my own past and the process through which I became a Jungian analyst. There was a time when suicide seemed an attractive alternative to the life I had.

Norman is in the fire. He is a broken man. He has all the symptoms of a midlife crisis: anxiety, depression, self-pity and guilt; he can't eat and he can't sleep; he has no energy and he's confused. Just about the only thing Norman has going for him is that he realizes he has a problem.

It is true that he doesn't yet understand the nature or the extent of his problem, but clearly he's at the end of his tether. He is a promising candidate for analysis precisely because he is on his knees.

Norman and his wife have a symbiotic relationship which both may stray from but not leave. Norman's family is his center; without it he could not exist. He feels rejected by his wife but there's nothing he can do about it; however miserable he feels, he sees no possibility of life without her. He cannot clearly assess his situation because whenever he thinks about it he is flooded with emotion.

I see a man all askew, split between head and body, mind and heart—much like the Miro painting on the cover of this book.

In terms of the development of neurosis outlined in the introduction, Norman's libido has ceased to progress. He is barely able to function. His environmental circumstances have changed, but he is not able to adapt. Feeling doesn't work and he can't think straight. His energy has regressed, activating infantile fantasies of a lost paradise—a good feeling relationship with his wife. To reestablish that he is eager to change.

There is an underground conflict raging in Norman. He is not yet aware of this, but were it not there he would not have been crying for several days and subsequently found his way to me. At this point, however, all his defenses are mobilized to prevent him from realizing that life as he has known it is finished. He only wants to "make things right," which would mean turning back the clock to when he felt loved.

Norman is paying a fair amount of money to see me. He came looking for help. He wants a solution to his problem and he genuinely believes I can provide it. But if I knew what Norman should do I would be God. Happily I am no longer able to indulge in that degree of inflation.

I listen to Norman and say nothing. I see his tears. I hear his pain. I feel no sympathy but I am not unaffected. The emotional chaos he is presenting has a peculiar effect on me. On the one hand, it leaves me quite cold; on the other, I feel a growing knot in my own stomach. Norman begins to interest me. We are brothers under the skin. His outer situation is not the same as mine was at his age, but our psychology is not so different. I could be seeing and hearing myself twenty years ago.

At that time I shared the widespread belief that analysis is a cure to which one submits for a certain time and then is discharged healed. This is a fantasy many people still have. It is left over from the early days of psychoanalysis when it was thought that the unconscious contained only repressed contents, and once these were made conscious and relived (abreacted) one would live happily ever after.

Alas, the unconscious turns out to be inexhaustible. Like a swimmer in the ocean, we may skim the waves, but something new is constantly rising up from the depths. As in the psyche, so in life: we are constantly faced with the necessity of adapting to new circumstances.

I know that Norman has an inappropriate attitude to his situation. I don't tell him this because he wouldn't know what I was talking about. He has to realize it himself; it has to grow on him like a rose in a bed of turnips. He has to suffer until he finds, or there wells up in him, an attitude that is better adapted to who he is and life as he finds it. For this he needs time. His suffering is the result of the conflict he is not yet conscious of. I know that any lasting solution is a result of intense suffering; it shows the degree to which one's life is intolerable. Just suffering, however, is not enough—you have to be willing to do something about it.

I say nothing to alleviate Norman's pain because at the moment he is right where he should be. He feels rotten but he has a chance to become conscious. Even if I were able to magic away his problem I would not.

Any conflict constellates the problem of opposites. Broadly speaking, "the opposites" refers to the ego and the unconscious. This is true whether the conflict is recognized as an internal one or not, since conflicts with other people, especially one's mate, are really externalizations of an unconscious conflict within oneself. Because they are not made conscious, they are acted out on others.

This is called projection, discussed in detail below, in chapter three. But here let us look at the psychology of conflict.

Whatever attitude exists in consciousness, the opposite is in the unconscious. There is no way to haul this out by force. If we try, it will refuse to come. That is why the process of analysis is unproductive unless there is an active conflict. As long as outer life proceeds relatively smoothly, there is no need to deal with the unconscious. When it doesn't, there's no way to avoid it; we are automatically confronted with the other side.

The classic conflict situation is one in which there is the possibility of, or temptation to, more than one course of action. Theoretically the options may be many. In practice a conflict is usually between two, each carrying its own chain of consequences.

Perhaps the most painful conflicts of all are those involving duty or a choice between security and freedom. Such conflicts generate a great deal of inner tension. As long as they are not conscious, the tension manifests as physical symptoms, particularly in the stomach,

the back and the neck. Conscious conflict, on the other hand
perienced as moral or ethical tension.

At the moment, Norman's problem is still in the stomach.

Conflict is a hallmark of neurosis, but conflict is not invariably
neurotic. Life naturally involves the collision between conflicting
obligations, incompatible desires. Decisions have to be made. Some
degree of conflict is even desirable since without a degree of tension
between the ego and the unconscious the flow of life is inhibited.
Conflict only becomes neurotic when it settles in and interferes with
the way one functions.

I used to have a fantasy when I had a conflict: somewhere there
was a big book of collective wisdom called *What To Do*. It contained
the prescribed solution to all life's problems. Whenever you found
yourself in a quandary you just had to look it up in the book and do
what it said. Such a fantasy comes from the father complex. If there
were a book like that, I wouldn't have to think for myself, I'd just do
what was laid down by tradition.

In reality, the serious problems have only individual solutions.

Many minor conflicts are amenable to reason; they yield to a logically satisfying decision. Serious conflicts do not so easily disappear;
in fact they often arise precisely because of a one-sided rational attitude, and thus are more likely to be prolonged than solved by reason
alone. Where this is so, it is appropriate to ask, "But what do I
want?" This question aims to constellate the function of feeling—
which evaluates what something is worth to us—since a serious
conflict invariably involves a disparity between thinking and feeling.
If feeling is not a conscious participant in the conflict, it needs to be
introduced. The same may be said for thinking.

Jung's particular contribution to the psychology of conflict was to
point out that if a person can hold the tension between the conflicting
opposites, then eventually something will happen in the psyche to
effectively resolve the conflict. The outer circumstances may in fact
remain the same, but a change takes place in the individual. This
change, essentially irrational and unforeseeable, appears as a new attitude to both oneself and others; energy previously locked up in a

state of indecision is released and movement becomes possible. Jung calls this the transcendent function, because what happens transcends the conflicting opposites.

At that point, it is as if you were to stand on a mountain top watching a raging storm below—the storm may go on, but you are outside of it; you are to some extent objective, no longer emotionally involved. There is a sense of peace.

This process requires patience and a strong ego, otherwise the tension cannot be held and a decision will be made out of desperation, just to escape the tension. Unfortunately that changes nothing, because when a decision is made prematurely—when the tension has not been held long enough—then the other side, the option that was not chosen, will be constellated even more strongly and you're right back in the fire.

Norman is like a formless puddle of water, uncontained. There is no way to tell if he will be able to hold the tension.

When a choice exists between two incompatible options, the psychological reality is that two separate personalities are involved. These may be thought of as different aspects of oneself or, more formally, as personifications of complexes.

Complexes are normal and present in everyone; there is no life without them because complexes are the building blocks of the personality, just as atoms and molecules are the invisible components of physical objects. We cannot get rid of complexes. The most we can do is become aware of how we are influenced by them and how they interfere with our conscious intentions. When we understand them, they lose their power to affect us. They do not disappear but over time their grip may loosen.

When I first went into analysis I knew nothing about complexes. I had heard the word, usually in a pejorative context, but I did not know what it meant. I had read something about the Oedipus complex, which seemed to have something to do with killing your father so you could have your mother all to yourself.

Some months later, after reading a good deal of Jung, I had an excellent knowledge of complexes. I had learned that they were essentially "feeling-toned ideas" that over the years accumulated around certain images, for instance "mother" and "father." I also knew they had an archetypal core: behind emotional associations with the personal mother, say, there was the mother archetype—a collective image of nourishment and security on the one hand (the positive mother), and devouring possessiveness on the other (the negative mother).

I still did not connect complexes with my own life and what they had to do with finding myself desperate.

When I was a student in Zurich, training to be an analyst, we were required to do the Word Association Experiment. This "test" was developed by Jung to illustrate how unconscious factors could disturb the workings of consciousness.

There is a list of one hundred words, to which you are asked to respond with what first comes into your head. The person conducting the experiment measures the delay in responding (the response time) with a stop watch.

"Head"—"bed" (0.8 sec.)
"Marry"—"together" (1.7 sec.)
"Woman"—"friend" (2 sec.)
"Home"—(long pause) "none" (5.6 sec.)

—and so on.

Then you go through the list a second time, noting different responses to the same words. Finally you are asked for comments on those words to which you had a longer-than-average response time, a merely mechanical response or a different association on the second run-through; all these, and a few others, had been flagged by the questioner as "complex indicators."

It was an illuminating experience. It was also deflating. It convinced me that I was not master in my own house, that complexes were not only real but were alive in me and quite autonomous, independent of my will. I realized they could affect my memory, my thoughts, my moods, my behavior. I was not free to be me—there *was* no "me"—when I was in a complex.

Freud described dreams as the *via regia* to the unconscious; Jung showed that the royal road to the unconscious was rather the complex, the architect of both dreams and symptoms.

Whenever a strong emotion is present—whether it be love or hate or sadness or joy—a complex has been activated. When we are emotional we cannot think straight, we hardly know how we feel. We speak and act out of the complex, and when it has run its course we wonder what took over.

Life would be very dull without complexes, that's true. But they drain our energy. Instead of sound judgment and an appropriate feeling response there is a void. Complexes fill that void with acrimony, resentment, irritation, self-pity, anxiety, fear and guilt. As long as we are unconscious, we are prone to being overwhelmed, possessed, driven, by one complex or another. That is the situation in neurosis.

Norman is certainly complexed. Otherwise he would not have a conflict and would not be in pain. Something—or someone, if we continue with the notion of personifying the complexes—is preventing him from making a decision that would change his situation and restore his peace of mind.

Which complex is driving Norman? I don't know for sure, but it isn't my job to identify what he's caught in, it's his. The regression of his energy has activated a grab-bag of complexes. It may take him years to differentiate one from another. In the meantime, I wouldn't lose my shirt if I bet on an active mother complex. I wouldn't win any prizes either.

Norman is so deeply embedded in the world of appearances and projection that I see him as Theseus in King Midas' maze. Where is the ball of thread that would allow him to get out? What is the task Norman will not, or cannot, accomplish?

This is all in my mind, of course. Norman hurts but does not feel trapped and he does not know mythology. But when he sneaks into the basement to have a joint he often thinks of suicide.

Meanwhile, Norman is telling me, for about the third time, how much his family means to him. He is indissolubly wed. I do not disbelieve him. Norman sees himself as a family man and a responsible father, and so he is in spite of his philandering. He has a lot of energy invested in life as he knows it. In spite of how awful he feels, he is scared to death of being without his wife and kids. He wouldn't know what to do without them. Norman sees this as being strongly committed to his family, for that is his persona.

Norman's wife is having an affair with another man, but he is determined to put up with it because he is civilized and rational. That is persona. He would not knowingly begrudge his wife something she needs that he cannot provide. That too is persona. The last thing he would ever do is abandon his wife and children over such a minor point as sexual incompatibility. That is also persona.

Many years before I went into analysis I was caught up in being a struggling writer. That was my persona, the way I thought of myself and how I presented myself to other people. I could not imagine life without this image of myself. More accurately, I did not exist outside of it. And so for several years I typed away in a small shed at the foot of the garden, identifying with every other struggling writer who had ever lived. I was disappointed that no one would publish what I wrote, but at the same time I exulted, anticipating the day when I would be discovered. I have lost this persona along the way, but I remember what it felt like.

Jung describes the persona as an aspect of the collective psyche, which means there is nothing individual about it. It may *feel* individual—quite special and unique, in fact—but the designations "struggling writer," for instance, and "father," "teacher," "doctor," are on the one hand simply social identities, and on the other ideal images. They do not describe a particular person; they do not distinguish one doctor or father or teacher or writer from any other.

Any persona has certain attributes and behavior patterns associated with it, as well as collective expectations to live up to: a struggling writer, for instance, is a serious thinker, on the brink of recognition; a teacher is a figure of authority, dedicated to imparting knowledge; a doctor is wise, versed in the arcane mysteries of the body; a priest is close to God, morally impeccable; a mother loves her children, she would sacrifice her life for them; an accountant is a whiz with figures but unemotional, and so on.

That is why we experience a sense of shock when we read of a teacher accused of molesting a student, a doctor charged with drug abuse, an alcoholic priest, a mother who drowns her child, or an accountant who fiddles the books to pay gambling debts.

In Norman's case, a family man does not leave his family.

The development of a collectively suitable persona always involves a compromise between what we know ourselves to be and what is expected of us as social beings, including a degree of courtesy and innocuous behavior.

There is nothing intrinsically wrong with a persona. Originally the word meant a mask worn by actors to indicate the role they played. On this level, it is an asset in mixing with other people. It is also useful as a protective covering. Close friends may know us for what we are; the rest of the world knows only what we choose to show them. Indeed, without an outer layer of some kind, we are simply too vulnerable. Only the foolish and naive attempt to move through life without a persona.

However, we must be able to drop our persona in situations where it is not appropriate. This is especially true in intimate relationships. There is a difference between myself as a Jungian analyst and who I am when I'm not practicing. The doctor's skill at heart surgery is little comfort to a neglected mate. The teacher's knowledge of the learning process does not impress his teenage son who wants to borrow the car. The wise preacher leaves his collar and his rhetoric at home when he goes courting.

By handsomely rewarding the persona, the outside world invites us to identify with it. Money, respect and power come to those who can perform single-mindedly and well in a social role. No wonder we are liable to forget that our essential identity is something other than the work we do, our function within the collective. From being a useful convenience, therefore, the persona easily becomes a trap.

It is one thing to realize this, quite another to do something about it. The poet Rilke put it quite well:

2

The Serpent Wakes

"Alas," said the mouse, "the world is growing smaller every day. At the beginning it was so big that I was afraid, I kept running and running, and I was glad when at last I saw walls far away to the right and left, but these long walls have narrowed so quickly that I am in the last chamber already, and there in the corner stands the trap that I must run into."
"You only need to change direction," said the cat, and ate it up.
—Franz Kafka, "A Little Fable."

Norman arrived in a new suit. He was quite chipper.

"I thought I deserved something special," he said. "It's like a new beginning. I've been feeling terrific all week, looking forward to coming back. I told Nancy I came to see you. She was really pissed off!" He grinned sheepishly.

" 'Why didn't you tell me you were going?' she said. I apologized. I could see she was really hurt. I don't blame her. I think it's the first time since we met that I've made a decision on my own. We decide everything together, what groceries to buy, what films to see, what I should wear to call on a new account."

Norman smiled. "Nancy's always been a big help to me. Did I tell you about our great dinner parties? She's a wonderful cook. Always the gracious hostess. She has a very keen mind, too. That's one of the things that attracted me to her, her strong opinions. She has an opinion on just about everything—politics, how to fix a lock, how to bring up kids, you name it. She'll tell me anything I need to know. I don't have to think at all."

He laughed and then stopped. "It's pretty irritating sometimes, like when I do a job around the house. She always knows how to do it better. I have a kind of standing joke with her—if you wanted a handyman you shoulda married one. I don't remember claiming to be handy. And if I did, I didn't mean with a hammer and saw."

Norman looked uncomfortable, as if he'd just spilled the beans.

"Anyway, Nancy was quite concerned about me seeing you. 'What did you tell him?' she said. I told her what we talked about— well, most of it—and said she shouldn't worry. 'Does he want to see me?' I told her I didn't think it was necessary, at least not yet. What do you think?"

I reminded Norman that I didn't work with couples.

"We thought of marriage counseling last year. We talked it all over. Nancy said she'd do what I wanted if it would help me feel better, but since our marriage is okay she didn't see much point in it. I mean we don't fight or anything. We're never mean to each other. I agreed with her. What do you think?"

I inclined my head.

"I cut down on the grass this week. Didn't seem to want it. Played with the kids, got back into my work, made a few contacts. I really have a good life."

Norman thought for a minute, his head bowed. "We haven't made love for awhile. I'm not pressing it. Hell, I know she feels bad about the situation. It must be pretty hard on her. Sometimes she cries at night. I thought I'd wait till she comes to me."

We spent the rest of the hour getting to know each other. Norman was a sales manager with a multinational corporation. The work he did was new to me and I listened attentively. He went on at length. I pressed him for details. He was confident and spoke with authority. He traveled out of town several times a month. He stayed in hotels and occasionally he met a woman. Sometimes they spent the night together. It wasn't a big deal, said Norman.

"You know how it is. I'm pretty vulnerable." He laughed. "I can't say no."

Norman grew up in northern Manitoba, a small town called Churchill, founded by fur trappers. It's about 1500 miles north of the border between Canada and the States. It's where the trees end and the tundra begins. The subsoil there is permanently frozen.

"Paralysis of the limbs starts early in the north," said Norman, "spreads quickly to the brain and vital organs. That's why I left after high school."

I liked his sense of humor. I thought we'd get along just fine.

I shook hands with Norman at the door. He was about to go when he turned back.

"Oh, by the way, I had a dream the other night. I was with my mother in a burning house. I was trying to put the fire out with a bucket but it had a hole in it. I couldn't find Nancy anywhere. I ran around in a panic. I started opening pop bottles and throwing them up to people on the burning roof, shouting, "If we don't put it out at the top we're fucked!"

"What do you say to that?" said Norman.

I thought about it. "I'll see you next week," I said.

*

Norman is experiencing an elation that is characteristic of how you feel after baring your soul to a professional for the first time. It has something to do with admitting defeat, acknowledging the inability to cope. Last week he said things to me that he'd never said to anyone else. That relieved some of the pressure that had built up.

This week he doesn't look or talk like a man who has any problem at all. Now, as far as he's concerned, it's all in my hands.

He is also a bit inflated, which automatically happens when the conscious mind takes on too many unconscious contents. You get puffed up with the new knowledge. Life is wonderful. Everything seems clear as a bell.

Both the high spirits and the inflation are usually temporary.

After my first hour of analysis I went out and got drunk. I was so happy! I couldn't believe the difference. I crawled in and I skipped out. I had no idea why. I can't recall now what I talked about that first time, but I remember feeling a lot better. The depression had gone. I called some friends and we partied all night.

Coming down from these highs is not much fun. Maybe that's why I don't like heights.

I have a strong urge to suggest to Norman that he keep what we talk about to himself, but I don't. He will know when this becomes necessary—if it does, and without any hint from me—and at this point he couldn't do it anyway. He believes that seeing me will bring him closer to his wife and for all I know it will. But he secretly feels proud of himself for making a decision without her.

Keeping secrets is very important in the analytic process. It intensifies what is going on inside. When you tell people other than your analyst what you're experiencing, something precious leaks out. It relieves the tension but slows down the process.

In the first months of analysis I was like a sieve. I couldn't keep anything to myself. I was living in Zurich with a man who was also a training candidate. Arnold and I hashed over everything: what we read, what we felt, our fantasies, our dreams and so on; we recreated our analytic sessions in detail, suggesting why our analysts said this or that—or smiled and said nothing—into the wee hours. It was a great time and we are still close because of it.

After a time my analyst said, "Look, you dream of bottles breaking and sinks overflowing; there's sand running through your fingers and water seeping out holes in the wall. What's that all about?"

I didn't know then, but I soon found out.

Arnold and I were caught up in a shared secret. Between us we had established a *participation mystique*—a situation in which we identified with each other's triumphs and misfortunes. That is the common cement of friendship and it has its place. I think I could not have survived those first months in Zurich without it, but our very closeness became a hindrance to what we were there to do: to confront ourselves, without support or judgment from another, to deal absolutely on our own with the impossible conflicts and contradictions we were experiencing.

In the beginning, neither of us had a container for such a task. We acted out our emotions; we dumped on, and contaminated, our surroundings.

There is an analogy in alchemy: the *vas Hermetis,* the hermetic vessel. It must be kept closed to allow the contents to transform through the application of heat. If the heat escapes, nothing happens. Psychologically this is like dissipating the tension of a conflict. The gold, the philosopher's stone, doesn't materialize. You're left with the same old lead you started with.

I was obliged, then, to create an inner temenos, a sacred space that was entirely my own. This heats up the psyche, heightens the tension. When you get used to the importance of a container you instinctively know what you can let out and what you can't. And when you make a mistake you can almost hear the temenos crack.

Of course I had my analyst. That relationship was another kind of temenos, a place where the gods could safely play in an atmosphere of mutual trust and respect. He observed and monitored my process; I relied on him to throw light on my dreams, to be there as a mirror, to keep me on track, but he was not intrusive. I often thought of him as a midwife, assisting at a birth.

He was crucial to the process, but in time, as my own temenos became less fragile, I didn't need to tell him everything.

Norman is virtually incapable of keeping anything from his wife. He feels guilty when he does. True, he has a selective memory, but on the whole he tells her what is going on in his head. This is a measure of his attachment to her and his need for approval—their shared *participation mystique.* He would like to be completely transparent, an open book, to his wife. His escapades with other women are a notable exception. These he keeps even from himself.

His wife, meanwhile, has a secret she is very concerned to keep. She has a lover. If Norman finds out it would ruin everything. The façade they have created, their whole house of cards, would collapse. (She doesn't know that Norman already knows. He can't tell her because he's sure to get a lickin' for snooping in her things.)

For years Norman's wife has lived stoically with his covert infidelity, not because she doesn't mind but because she has no choice. She is as tied to the relationship as Norman is. She has too much to lose if he cracks. She is quite sure he couldn't stand it if he knew what she was up to. That's why she doesn't admit to it. She doesn't know he's already cracked.

Norman's wife is at once the protective mother, genuinely concerned for her son-husband's peace of mind, and a conniving witch who will do what she wants but at all costs preserve what she has. Like Norman, she wants to have her cake and eat it too.

How do I know what is going on in Norman's wife? Because I have worked analytically with her sisters—the wives and girlfriends of men like Norman. The details are always different, but the psychological pattern is the same. They hide themselves to protect their men from the pain of growing up. They live tormented, schizophrenic lives, close to the brink, until they relinquish their identification with the mother.

That's the way I see it, but I might be wrong.

Norman thinks his wife does him a favor by allowing him to make love to her. He stews, waiting for her to be overwhelmed by desire. He is entirely at the mercy of her whims. He just wants to be loved, which he equates with desire, and more specifically his wife's desire for him. As long as she is indifferent, he doesn't feel loved. Other women may desire him, and show it, but since they are not his wife this does not affect the equation in his head. He still doesn't feel loved.

Norman is suffering because he is emotionally committed to a woman he experiences as unloving.

He knows nothing of his wife's fears, her needs, her complexes. He does not understand her crying in the night. Perhaps when he is in the basement, having a toke, she is in the attic, eating her heart out. None of this occurs to Norman. He is too caught up in himself to think about what's going on in her.

Of course he sympathizes with her plight—not being sexually interested in your husband must be awful—but he sees it as his fault. That is the influence of his mother complex, aptly symbolized by the cat in the passage that opens this chapter, an imprisoning trap that effectively prevents a man from "changing direction," reorienting his conscious attitude.

I remember a remark by my first analyst: "By our compassion we are unmanned."

Norman is not very comfortable discussing his wife, or their relationship, with me. It feels disloyal, as if he were betraying a confidence. They have always been a team. Their marriage is his center, his temenos. How will he deal with the conflict when he becomes aware of the growing need in him for some psychological distance from his mate?

Norman thinks he knows what he wants: a loving wife. But in fact he wants a mother, a safe place to come home to. Nancy is in a pretty pickle. On the one hand he is her devoted son-lover, a situation that feels like incest to her and inhibits her desire. On the other, she would genuinely like to be there for him when he comes home. Maybe that's why she is eating her heart out in the attic—if she is.

And thirdly, perhaps unknown to her, she enjoys the power.

I don't know Norman's wife. I know only what he tells me about her. I know that much of this is in his mind and has nothing to do with his wife. Norman does not yet know there is a difference. I certainly don't want to see her because I am only interested in how Norman experiences his wife, not who she really is. To meet her would just confuse me.

That is the difference between individual analysis and working with couples.

At this point I have an opinion about Norman's situation and a good idea of what he should do about it. But it would be a great disservice to him if I were to express this. It would be interfering with his own process, and even if by some lucky chance I hit the nail on the head he is not ready to hear it.

Norman's dream, imparted as an afterthought, is in any case much more relevant than my opinion, or indeed his wife's. It tells us where he is rather than where I think he is, or should be.

An initial dream—the first dream one brings to an analytic session—is of special significance because it often shows both the underlying factors responsible for bringing a person into analysis and the essential psychological problems that need to be worked through.

These may only be apparent in hindsight; perhaps not until years later is that first dream's symbolic content recognized for what it meant at the time. But it always carries a numinosity, a particular fascination or feeling quality, that cannot be denied. One keeps coming back to it as a reference point.

I never had any dreams before I went into analysis. At least I never remembered them. That's not quite true. When I was six I fell asleep on the toilet and dreamed God came and told me everything would be alright. And I recall some other childhood dreams of beautiful gardens peopled with elves and fairies.

My first degree was in maths and physics. Dreams were not mentioned. Then I studied journalism. As a reporter, I got to cover political speeches. They were full of dreams, but of another kind. Even when I returned to university to study literature and philosophy I never heard it suggested that dreams might be important.

According to research into the physiology of dreaming we all dream, several times a night, shown by so-called REM phenomena— rapid eye movements. People deprived of the level of sleep at which dreams occur soon become anxious and irritable. These experiments, while silent about the content or meaning of dreams, suggest they have an important biological function.

Jung went further: he believed the purpose of dreams was to monitor and regulate the flow of energy in the psyche.

As an adult I must have had dreams, then, but for lack of attention they died in the water. Why would I be interested in dreams anyway? They happen at night and have nothing to do with me.

That's what I thought until I woke up one morning with a dream that wouldn't go away.

My initial dream, the one that took me into analysis, was of a bouncing ball. I was on a street in the center of a deserted city, surrounded by cavernous buildings. I was bouncing a ball between the buildings, from one side to another. It kept getting away from me, I could not pin it down. I woke up in a cold sweat, terrified, sobbing uncontrollably.

From this distance it seems quite innocuous. At the time it blew my whole world apart.

It was my introduction to the reality of the psyche, a kind of initiation, a baptism by fire. I did not know that something could be going on in me without me being aware of it. I believed that will power could accomplish anything. "Where there's a will there's a way." My dream came in the midst of a mighty conflict which I had a will to solve but no way. I kept thinking I could deal with it by myself. My reaction to the dream killed that illusion.

The psyche is the sum total of all psychic processes, conscious as well as unconscious. Psychic phenomena are as real as anything in the physical world. The unconscious is quite independent of consciousness; it not only reacts to consciousness and contains repressed contents that were once conscious, it is also the source for things that have never been conscious—it can create.

Jung describes dreams as fragments of involuntary psychic activity, just conscious enough to be reproducible in the waking state. They are self-portraits, symbolic statements of what is going on in the personality from the point of view of the unconscious.

Knowledge of oneself is a result of looking in two directions at once. In order to know ourselves we need both relationships with other people and the mirror of the unconscious. Dreams provide that mirror.

Dreams are independent, spontaneous manifestations of the unconscious. Their message seldom coincides with the tendencies of the conscious mind. They not only fail to obey our will, but often stand in flagrant opposition to our conscious attitudes and intentions. They are not more important than what goes on during the day, but they are helpful comments on our outer existence.

Freud's view was that dreams have an essentially wish-fulfilling and sleep-preserving function. Jung acknowledged this to be true in some cases but focused on the prominent role dreams play in the self-regulation of the psyche. He suggested that their main function was to compensate conscious attitudes—to call attention to different points of view, and in so doing to produce an adjustment in the ego-personality.

Compensation is a process aimed at establishing or maintaining balance in the psyche. If the conscious attitude is too one-sided, the dream takes the opposite tack; if the conscious attitude is more or less appropriate, the dream seems satisfied with pointing out minor variations; and if the conscious attitude is entirely adequate, then the dream may even coincide with and support it.

Dreams have a compensatory function in that they reveal aspects of the personality that are not normally conscious; they disclose unconscious motivations operating in relationships and they present new points of view in conflict situations.

Jung also emphasized the prospective or purposive function of dreams, which means that in many cases their symbolic content outlines the solution of a conscious conflict. This is in line with his view of neurosis as purposeful: the aim of dreams is to present to consciousness the information needed to restore the psyche to health.

"If that's true," I said to my analyst, "if they're really that important, then why are they so damned hard to understand?"

He just smiled.

Jung's equally enigmatic answer is that "the dream is a natural occurrence, and . . . nature shows no inclination to offer her fruits gratis or according to human expectations."[1]

It takes hard work to understand dreams. We aren't used to their symbolic language. The combination of ideas in dreams is essentially fantastic and irrational; images are linked together in a way that as a rule is quite foreign to our usual linear way of thinking. At first sight they often make very little sense. And at second sight too. The language of dreams certainly takes some getting used to.

One of my dreams after I started analysis in Zurich was of a spider on skis, on a razor blade. Now I ask you. And people say the unconscious has no sense of humor.

---

[1] "On the Nature of Dreams," *The Structure and Dynamics of the Psyche,* CW 8, par. 560.

According to Jung, a dream is an interior drama. The dreamer is the stage, the scene, the director, the author, the actors, the audience and the critic. The dream is the dreamer. Each element in a dream refers to an aspect of the dreamer's own personality; in particular, the people in dreams are personifications of complexes.

Dreams confront us with our complexes and show them at work in determining our attitudes, which are in turn responsible for much of our behavior. The work required to understand the message of a dream, or a series of dreams, is one of the best ways to depotentiate the complexes because through this focused attention we establish a conscious relationship to them.

Our own dreams are particularly difficult to understand because our blind spots—our complexes—always get in the way to some extent. Even Jung, after working on thousands of dreams over a period of fifty years, confessed to this frustration. A rule of thumb is that if you think you understand a dream right off the bat, you've missed the point.

Freud was the first to suggest that it is not possible to interpret a dream without the cooperation of the dreamer. You need a thorough knowledge of the outer situation at the time of the dream, and the conscious attitude. This, and personal associations to the images in the dream, can only come from the dreamer. If the essential purpose of a dream is to compensate conscious attitudes, you have to know what these are or the dream will forever remain a mystery.

The exception to this is archetypal dreams. These are distinguished by the presence of symbolic images and motifs common to myths and religions all over the world. They commonly appear at times of great emotional crisis, when one is experiencing a situation that involves a more or less universal human problem. They tend to occur in transitional periods of life, when a change in the conscious attitude is imperative.

Norman's initial dream is archetypal. So was mine.

There is no fixed meaning to symbols or motifs in dreams, no valid interpretation that is independent of the psychology and life situation of the dreamer. Thus the routine recipes and stereotyped "definitions" found in traditional dream books are of no value whatever.

I am looking at a thick paperback entitled *Ten Thousand Dreams Interpreted, or What's in a Dream: A Scientific and Practical Exposition*.[2] Published over fifty years ago, it is still widely available. Here are some of the entries:

"To dream of seeing your home burning denotes a loving companion, obedient children, and careful servants."

"To dream of bananas foretells that you will be mated to an uninteresting and unloved companion."

"You will usually find after dreaming of salt that everything goes awry, and quarrels and dissatisfactions show themselves in the family circle."

"To dream of thick, unsightly lips signifies disagreeable encounters, hasty decision, and ill temper in the marriage relation."

"Carving meat denotes bad investments, but, if a change is made, prospects will be brighter."

Books like this are fun to read but no help to the serious student of dreams. Nor are fatuous claims that we can control our dreams—consciously manipulate their content. There is no convincing evidence that this is possible, nor would it be desirable even if it were, for one would thereby lose valuable information that is not available otherwise.

Many dreams have a classic dramatic structure. There is an *exposition* (place, time and characters), which shows the initial situation of the dreamer. In the second phase there is a *development* in the plot (action takes place). The third phase brings the *culmination* or climax (a decisive event occurs). The final phase is the *lysis,* the result or solution of the action in the dream. It is often helpful to look at the lysis as showing where the dreamer's energy wants to go. Where there is no lysis, no solution is in sight.

The best way to work on one's dreams is in a dialogue with another person, preferably someone trained to look at dreams objec-

---

[2] Gustavus Hindman Miller (Northbrook, Il: Hubbard Press, 1931).

tively and not likely to project his or her own psychology onto the dream. Even an analytic knowledge of one's own complexes is no guarantee against projection, but without training of some kind both parties are in the soup.

The first step is to get the personal associations to all the images in the dream. If there is a tree, say, or a rug or a snake or apple, it is important to determine what these mean in the experience of the dreamer. This takes the form of circumambulating the image, which means staying close to it: "What does a snake mean to you?" . . . "What else?" . . . "And what else?" This is not the same as the traditional Freudian method of free association, which eventually gets to the complex but may miss the significance of the image.

On top of personal associations to dream images there are often relevant amplifications—what trees or rugs or snakes or apples have meant to other people in other cultures at other times.

These are called archetypal associations; they serve to broaden conscious awareness by bringing in material that is not personally known but is present in the unconscious as part of everyone's psychic heritage. The same images and motifs that turn up in dreams are the substance of myths, religions and fairy tales. Hence a working knowledge of these is an integral part of an analyst's training.[3]

Garnering personal and archetypal associations to a dream—examining its context—is a relatively simple, almost mechanical, procedure. It is necessary but only preparation for the real work, the actual interpretation of the dream and what it is saying about the dreamer's life and conscious attitudes. This is an exacting task and an experience so intimate that the understanding of any particular dream is really only valid for the two persons working on it.

That is why a person in analysis should be wary of discussing with a friend or mate the meaning of a dream arrived at with the ana-

---

[3] Jung's *Collected Works* and Marie-Louise von Franz's writings on fairy tales and alchemy are particularly helpful in understanding archetypal images and motifs. Also valuable is Fraser Boa's film series with von Franz, published as *The Way of the Dream* (Toronto: Windrose Films, 1988).

lyst. To attempt to describe the ineffable to a third person who is not privy to the intimate associations of the dream risks undermining a hard-won personal standpoint. It may also interfere with the temenos being established with the analyst.

Dreams may be interpreted on a subjective or an objective level. The former approach considers a dream strictly in terms of the dreamer's own psychology. If a person I know appears in my dream, the focus is not on that actual person but on him or her as an image or symbol of projected unconscious contents. Where I have a vital connection with that person, however, an objective interpretation may be more to the point—the dream is saying something about the relationship between us.

In either case, the image of the other person derives from my own psychology. But whether a subjective or objective approach is more valid has to be determined from the context of the dream and the personal associations.

Dreams invariably have more than one meaning. Ten analysts can look at a dream and come up with ten different interpretations, depending on their typology and their own complexes. That is why there is no valid interpretation without dialogue, and why the dreamer must have the final say. What "clicks" for the dreamer is the "right" interpretation—for the moment, because subsequent events, and later dreams, often throw new light on previous dreams . . .

What are we to make, then, of my bouncing ball dream and the one Norman left me with on the doorstep?

In the first place, as already indicated, both are typical of the kind of dream one has in a midlife crisis, when a change in conscious attitudes is imperative. Personal associations are not crucial because their meaning is more or less transparent. With a minimal knowledge of archetypal motifs, they reveal the psychology of the dreamer at the time of the dream, whether one knows the dreamer's outer circumstances or not.

In my dream, the difficulty is clearly one of keeping the opposites in balance. My center is pictured as being in a city, a collective space. A ball, compared to anything else that naturally occurs in nature, contains the largest internal volume for a given surface area. It cannot contain more without splitting the surface—or the surface must expand in order to contain more. It is a thus a symbol for both self-containment and the self-regulating process in the psyche. The ball keeps getting away from me. The compensating message of the dream is that I am not in control. Perhaps, if I could establish a personal center, if I could become more contained . . .

In Norman's dream, he finds himself in a burning house. The house is his personal psychic space. The raging fire is the affect constellated by his conflict. It threatens to consume him unless he deals with it. His mother is present but his wife is not. His mother has been dead for some years but her image, what "mother" means to him, is very much alive in his psychology. A bucket is a container. Norman's container is not suited to the task; it has a hole in it, reflecting his difficulty in keeping things to himself. Containers are archetypally associated with the feminine; this side of Norman, his anima, is in cahoots with the mother.

The pop bottles suggest an adolescent attitude, the people on the roof his expectation that others will do the work. The burning roof puts the conflict in his head.

The fact that Norman told me the dream when he was leaving and not when he came in shows that he has no conscious awareness of its relevance to his life situation. He is in danger and he doesn't know it. Fortunately the unconscious does; in the dream he is in a panic. That is the compensating message of the dream—to make him conscious of the dire straits he is in.

However ineffectual are Norman's efforts to put out the fire, at least the desire is there, as well as a sense of urgency. Putting out the fire can be seen as a metaphor for assimilating the complexes instead of being possessed by them. For this to happen, the conflict will have to move from being a merely intellectual problem to one that he experiences on a feeling level. Then, perhaps, he will be moved to do something about it.

The outcome of Norman's psychological situation is at this point problematical, for at least two reasons: 1) it is characteristic of the neurotic mind to note its suffering and take no action, and 2) Norman has no container independent of his wife and family.

Analysis involves a more or less thorough readjustment of the personality. To some extent this means separating from those collective attitudes and values that for a particular individual, in a particular context, do not work. There are collective attitudes and solutions that are appropriate to many situations, but people generally go into analysis precisely because there is no satisfactory collective answer to what they are going through.

At the moment, Norman is wrapped in a cloak he picked up somewhere along the line. He needs an answer that is right for him. He has no idea what that might be, nor do I.

I did not tell Norman any of this because our hour was up and I like to keep on time.

3

The Unknown Other

Anyone who has unconscious assumptions must be treated like an insane person: one must let him have them until he comes into conflict with himself.

—C.G. Jung, *Letters.*

Norman came in rather subdued. He had been out late the night before and was quite hung over. I poured us each a glass of ice water, my usual routine.

"I don't know what gets into me," he said. "I have good intentions, I'm tired and ready to go home, and then I get talking to some chick and I could stay up all night. It's just very exciting, I guess."

He laughed self-consciously. "This girl came on to me, what's her name, Penny. We had a great time after the party. I took her home and we made love until the sun came up. Her husband is in the navy, he's at sea for a few weeks. She doesn't seem to miss him, at least she's not up-tight about being married. Anyway, she liked being with me."

It's the rake-hell talking.

"I wish Nancy was so . . . so free." He ran his fingers through his hair. "Well, with me, I mean. Making love to her is like playing bridge with a zombie. Just hold the cards, I think to myself—you need a partner or you can't play, right?"

Back to the mother.

"How did you meet your wife?" I asked.

Norman beamed.

"It was magic. I saw her and I fell in love! I was completely besotted. I couldn't get her out of my mind. She'd been a cheerleader, there were a dozen other guys after her. I really had to fight for Nancy. She was very popular, she could pick and choose.

"In those days she sure liked making love, we did it everywhere. Once she laughed at me when I was too tired. I said to her, jokingly, 'You're insatiable.' 'I thought men never got enough,' she said. 'They're always talking about women who like it all the time.'"

He grinned weakly. "That hurt me, somehow. It got me thinking about the men she'd known before me. I didn't like to hear about her past."

I felt the knot in my stomach.

"I was desperate to marry Nancy. But she said she wasn't ready for a long-term relationship. Then she got pregnant; her diaphragm didn't fit well, she said. Well, I was happy as anything. I loved her, there was nothing I wanted more than having our baby. She didn't say yes right away. I know she thought a lot about having a kid on her own. She was very independent in those days. But she finally agreed." Norman smiled.

"We had a small wedding, a few close friends. Nancy's father wasn't there, of course, he took off when she was four. But her uncle said some nice things about her. They were always very close. Her mother cried the whole time.

"The next few months were pretty bad. We stayed with her mother while we looked for a place to live. Nancy was depressed and slept a lot. She couldn't get around so easily anyway, so I would go out each morning and check out the ads."

He pulled out a handkerchief and blew his nose.

"It wasn't easy to find an apartment for what we could pay. I followed up all the leads. More than once I came back and cried on her lap. It was just too much. Once I put down a deposit on a couple of rooms above a grocery store. When I took Nancy to see it she said she couldn't live there, it was too depressing. It was true, the rooms were small, they smelled bad and there was no light. She finally got out of bed and found something better."

Norman looked at his feet. "After she had the baby everything changed. We got along okay, I mean I'd do anything to please her, but she wasn't very interested in screwing, you know? She never turned me down but she didn't . . . well, she wasn't . . ." He shrugged helplessly. "I guess maybe she never really liked it as much as I thought."

"I went on the road," said Norman. "I traveled quite a bit. It wasn't really necessary but it got me away from home. Nancy never minded me leaving, she was very loving when she kissed me good-by. 'Enjoy yourself,' she'd say. 'Have a good time!'

"As if I could. I couldn't be away for more than a few days without getting homesick. Sometimes I'd meet a woman but I just got so lonely without Nancy, I'd rush back. I could never really enjoy myself without her."

Norman shrugged. "I still can't."

*

This is our fourth session together. Some things are starting to fall together.

Norman has what is called a split anima. On the one hand there is the mother-type anima, an inner image of woman who represents stability and emotional security. This he projects onto his wife. On the other there is the free-wheeling, devil-take-the-hindmost anima, which he automatically projects onto any woman who is sexually available.

Norman is somewhere in between. However, the mother has the upper hand; he can go through the motions with another woman but he can't enjoy it.

Psychologically the anima functions in a man as his soul. Jung described it as the archetype of life. When a man is full of life he is "animated." The man with no connection to his soul feels dull and lifeless. Nowadays we call this depression—prime symptom of a midlife crisis—but the experience is not new. The primitive mind called it loss of soul.

I remember falling in love with the woman who later became my wife. We were in Paris at the time, halfway up the Eiffel Tower. It was very foggy. We huddled close and kissed. That was it, I was a goner. I actually jumped for joy.

It didn't work out between my wife and me, but I still dream of her. When we split up I went into a depression for about three years. I like the description of this as "loss of soul" because that's just what it feels like.

A man unconscious of his feminine side tends to be moody and sentimental—anima-possessed. By paying attention to his moods and emotional reactions, he can come into possession of his soul rather than be possessed by it.

Jung distinguished four broad stages of the anima in the course of a man's psychological development. He personified these as Eve, Helen, Mary and Sophia.

In the first stage, Eve, the anima is completely tied up with the mother—not necessarily the personal mother, but the image of mother as faithful provider of nourishment, security and love. The man with an anima of this type cannot function well without a vital connection to a woman and is easy prey to being controlled by her. He frequently suffers impotence or has no sexual desire at all.

In the second stage, personified in the historical figure of Helen of Troy, the anima is a collective sexual image. She is Marlene Dietrich, Marilyn Monroe, Tina Turner, all rolled up into one. The man under her spell is often a Don Juan who engages in repeated sexual adventures. These will invariably be short-lived, for two reasons: 1) he has a fickle heart—his feelings are whimsical and often gone in the morning—and 2) no real woman can live up to the expectations that go with this unconscious, ideal image.

The third stage of the anima is Mary. It manifests in religious feelings and a capacity for genuine friendship between the sexes. The man with an anima of this kind is able to see a woman as she is, independent of his own needs. His sexuality is integrated into his life, not an autonomous function that drives him. He can differentiate between love and lust. He is capable of lasting relationships because he can tell the difference between the object of his desire and his inner image of woman.

In the fourth stage, as Sophia (called Wisdom in the Bible), a man's anima functions as a guide to the inner life, mediating to consciousness the contents of the unconscious. Sophia is behind the need to grapple with the grand philosophical issues, the search for meaning. She is Beatrice in Dante's *Inferno,* and the creative muse in any artist's life. She is a natural mate for the "wise old man" in the male psyche. The sexuality of a man at this stage is naturally exuberant, since it incorporates a spiritual dimension.

Theoretically, a man's anima development proceeds through these various stages as he grows older. When the possibilities of one have been exhausted—which is to say, when adaptation to oneself and outer circumstances requires it—the psyche stimulates the move to the next stage.

In fact, the transition from one stage to another seldom happens without a struggle—if it takes place at all—for the psyche not only promotes and supports growth, it is also, paradoxically, conservative and loathe to give up what it knows. Hence a psychological crisis is commonly precipitated when there is a pressing need for a man to move from one stage to the next.

For that matter, a man may have periodic contact with any of these anima images, at any time of life, depending on what is required to compensate the dominant conscious attitude.

Norman, at the present time, is caught between Eve and Helen. When he looks at his wife he sees not Nancy but Eve. When he is caught up in a momentary attraction to another women he sees Helen. He has glimpses of Mary, his wife as an independent other—her life before he met her, for instance, which as a matter of fact terrifies him—but he is far from any contact with Sophia.

A man's inner image of woman is initially determined by his experience of the personal mother. It is later modified through contact with other women—relatives, teachers, etc.—but the experience of the personal mother is so powerful and long-lasting that a man is naturally attracted to those women who are much like her—or her direct opposite.

Any man who is unconscious of his feminine side is prone to see this aspect of himself, his soul, in an actual woman. The most common way to experience this is by falling in love. To understand it we have to look more closely at the concept of projection.

We are naturally inclined to believe that the world is as we see it, that people are who we imagine them to be. We soon learn that this is not so at all, because other people frequently turn out to be completely different from the way we thought they were. If they are not particularly close, we think no more about it. If it's an intimate friend, we are devastated.

Jung suggested that we are constantly projecting our own unconscious contents into our environment. We see unacknowledged aspects of ourselves in other people. In this way we create a series of imaginary relationships that often have little or nothing to do with the other person.

No one can escape this. It is the natural thing for unconscious contents to be projected. That is life. Projection has generally had a bad press, but in its positive sense it creates an agreeable bridge between people, facilitating friendship and communication. It greases the wheels. As with complexes, life would be a whole lot duller without projection.

You can also project onto things. This used to be known as a fetish and was generally considered to be unhealthy. People laughed at you if you had a fascination for, say, shoes or buttons. They still do, but now psychologists know that such things have an inner symbolic meaning.

One dreary afternoon I was walking in the hills of Zurich, feeling very sorry for myself, when I spied an object on the path. I stooped down and picked it up. It was a little black elephant made of ebony. It was numinous to me, a magical thing. I fell in love.

I took it to be a case of what Jung calls synchronicity, where what is happening outside coincides with an inner event.[1] I assumed it had something to do with my psychology and spent the next few years exploring what that could be.

---

[1] See "Synchronicity: An Acausal Connecting Principle," *The Structure and Dynamics of the Psyche,* CW 8.

I went to see elephants in the zoo, I read books about them, I collected them. I painted pictures of elephants, my dreams were full of them. Today I am surrounded by elephants of all sizes and materials and many household objects incorporating their shape, like coffee mugs, lamps, ashtrays, plant holders, letter-openers, baskets and even a dinner bell. I have a pretty good idea of the relevance of elephants to me and why I found that first one.

Here are a few little-known facts about elephants:

Queen Maya, the Buddha's mother, dreamed that a white elephant entered her womb the night she conceived the savior. (This is analogous to Mary's Annunciation in Christianity.)

In Kundalini yoga the elephant is the symbol for the *muladhara* chakra, the lowest spiritual center, located somewhere between the anus and the genitals. (It is particularly active, they say, when a person is depressed.)

An elephant has a penis six feet long, flaccid.

An old myth tells how elephants once could fly and change shape like clouds. One day a flock landed on the branch of a tree and killed a holy man. From that time on they were condemned to walk on land. (This is comparable to a person who was up in the air and then came down to earth. Maybe *that's* why I don't like heights.)

The most formidable enemy of the elephant is the snake, ubiquitous symbol for the unconscious. (I painted snakes too, and once I got an elephant and a snake to kiss.)

The other day I read about a man who has been hiding out for four years with two elephants. He brought them up from babies and sold them, but he believed they weren't being well cared for, so he took them back in the middle of the night and hasn't been seen since.

The newspaper quoted his daughter: "It's not easy hiding out with a couple of elephants standing six and seven feet tall. All I can say is my father is a very clever man."[2]

Yes indeed. And elephants are invisible. I added that to my list of little-known facts.

---

[2] *Toronto Globe and Mail,* March 28, 1988.

There is passive projection and there is active projection. Passive projection is completely automatic and unintentional. Our eyes catch another's across a crowded room and we are smitten, hopelessly in love. We may know nothing about that person; in fact the less we know the easier it is to project—we fill the void with ourselves.

Active projection is also called empathy. You feel yourself into the other's shoes by imagining what he or she is going through. This is an essential ability for an analyst. Without it there is a long succession of boring days with uninteresting people who have unimaginable problems. With it, you're on the edge.

There is a very thin line between empathy and identification. Identification presupposes no separation between subject and object, no difference between me and the other person. We are two peas in a pod. What is good for me must be good for him—or her. Many relationships run aground on this mistaken notion. It is the motivation for much well-meaning advice to others, and the premise of any therapeutic system relying on suggestion or adaptation to collective behavior and ideals.

Therapy conducted on this basis does more harm than good. That is why Jung insisted that those training to be analysts must have a thorough personal analysis before being let loose. Only through an intimate knowledge of my own complexes and predispositions can I know where I end and the other begins.

And even then I can't always be sure. When someone like Norman shows up, I really have to be careful.

In relationships, identification is as common as potatoes. It always spells trouble. When you identify with another person, your emotional well-being is intimately linked with the mood of that person and his or her attitude toward you. This easily becomes a clinging, sticky sentimentality.

I am grateful to my friend Arnold for the observation that the psychology of such a situation is succinctly expressed in that old popular song, "I Want To Be Happy, But I Can't Be Happy, Till I Make You Happy Too."

It's a classic double-bind. You can't function independently and your dependence has the effect of making the other person responsible for how *you* feel. More: you have a relationship that is psychologically no different from that between parent and child. Worse: at any given moment it is hard to tell which partner is parent and which is child.

We may gladly accept this responsibility toward our children, but between grownups it is in the long run unworkable. Neither can make a move without double-thinking the effect on the other; this greatly inhibits the self-expression of both.

Projection, if it doesn't go as far as identification, is actually quite useful. When we assume that some quality or characteristic is present in another, and then, through experience, find that this is not so, we are obliged to realize that the world is not our own creation. If we are reflective, we can learn something about ourselves.

This process is called withdrawing projections. It doesn't happen overnight and it's about as painful as you can get.

It only becomes necessary to withdraw projections when our expectations of others are frustrated. If there is no obvious disparity between what we expect, or imagine to be true, and the reality we are faced with, there is no need to withdraw projections. Don't look a gift horse in the mouth, let sleeping dogs lie—as long as they do.

I think about how all this applies to Norman.

Norman did not fall in love with Nancy. He fell in love with his own soul, in other words himself. At the time he met Nancy she was apparently a good hook for it: both a protective mother (Eve) and a willing sex partner (Helen). His attitude toward her has not changed. But Nancy has. No wonder he hurts. She has, in effect, refused to be his soul. Norman is stranded in a no-man's land. He is married to a woman who no longer embodies what he fell in love with.

I needn't point out to Norman that he has a projection on his wife, because something in him is pushing for that realization. In the meantime he's suffering, as I did, from loss of soul. The only antidote to this is to become aware of what he saw, and still sees, in his wife, and to measure this against his current experience of her.

True, he will still be without a soul. But at least he can stop expecting his wife to be what she isn't.

It is common when this happens to look for one's soul in another woman. I did it myself—about twenty times. I could fall in love at the drop of a hat. Arnold found this quite amazing.

"You poor sucker," he said, when yet again I came home with stars in my eyes, "how could you?"

"I love this one," I protested. "This is for real."

"Oh yeah?" he said, "tell me about it."

Arnold acknowledged that he was influenced by a negative mother complex. He looked at all women with suspicion, and particularly those I brought home. He saw ulterior motives whether they were there or not. Where I saw an angel he saw a witch. He once told me it was impossible for him to fall in love because he knew too much about himself.

"My anima is a cold-hearted slut," said Arnold, quite calmly.

When he finally did fall in love, it was with a soft, vivacious pixie. So much for compensation.

It is true, however, that a man under the thumb of a positive mother complex is vulnerable to women. His anima is undeniably starry-eyed, he sees women through rose-colored glasses. He genuinely likes women and is prone to identify with them. He seeks out their company because it feels good. Women think he understands them. He is often a charming lover, a Don Juan who can't say no. Typically he is also oversensitive, his feelings are easily hurt.

A man of this kind needs some conscious contact with his shadow, invariably a ruthless knave who, left to lurk in the unconscious, wreaks havoc on the hearts of unsuspecting women.

He could also use a rather tougher persona, like the thick skin of an elephant.

A positive mother complex inclines a man toward the ideal of togetherness. Although individual psychological development—individuation—is not possible without relationship, it is not compatible with togetherness. Individuation requires a focus on the inner axis, ego to unconscious. Togetherness blurs or obliterates the boundaries, because it aims at the commingling of one ego with another.

Individuation offers the basis for relating to another from a position of personal integrity. Togetherness represents fusion with another, the submersion of two individualities into one.

The "united front" that characterizes Norman's marriage is based on the ideal of togetherness. Norman identifies with his wife; his devotion to her is so strong that he sometimes forgets that he himself is dying. At the same time he is beginning to resent her. The tie is loosening, but it's still pretty tight. This is not surprising, since they have colluded for years in the fiction that they don't have any problems.

They don't fight or quarrel, not because they have no problems but because they don't reveal their true feelings to each other. They cannot do so because neither can stand disharmony.

If I were Norman I would take all his wife's clothes and rip them to shreds. "There," I would say, "now go out with your friend." That would show her how I felt. If I were his wife, I would beat Norman's head with a baseball bat.

That's just a personal fantasy.

I am far from feeling that Norman has to leave his wife. True, I am a bit cynical about wedded bliss, but if Norman can see his wife more realistically—if he can withdraw his projection—it might save their marriage. It depends on whether or not he likes what he sees, and if *she* can stand what he sees.

The outcome of Norman and Nancy's situation is not at all certain. The only thing I know is that whichever way he turns, I'll be the devil's advocate for the other direction. My job is to keep the conflict alive until he knows what he's doing and why.

There is nothing wrong with the way Norman initially experienced his wife. It was simply an indication of his psychology at the time. And hers, of course. Her attraction to him says something about her inner man, her animus, which naturally is, or at least was, projected onto Norman.

What did she see in him? What did she expect? The way Norman tells it, she was not "besotted," as he was, but she did agree to marry him. Why? Just because she was pregnant? I don't think so. I think she saw something in him that coincided with a need in her.

A woman's inner image of man is strongly colored by her experience of the personal father. Just as a man is apt to marry his mother, so to speak, so a woman is inclined to favor a man psychologically like her father; or, again, his opposite.

Whereas the anima in a man functions as his soul, a woman's animus is more like an unconscious mind. It manifests negatively in fixed ideas, unconscious assumptions and collective opinions that may be generally right but just beside the point in a given situation. An unconscious woman is always highly opinionated (animus-possessed). This kind of woman proverbially wears the pants, rules the roost—or tries to. She will drive a man to distraction on the one hand, and coldly emasculate him on the other.

A woman's animus becomes a helpful psychological factor only when she can tell the difference between "him" and herself. While a man's task in assimilating the anima involves discovering his true feelings, a woman must constantly question her ideas and opinions, measuring these against what she really thinks. If she does so, in time the animus can become a valuable inner companion who endows her with the positive masculine qualities of enterprise, courage, objectivity and spiritual wisdom.

Jung describes four stages of animus development in a woman, similar to the stages of the anima in a man. He first appears in dreams and fantasy as phallus, the embodiment of physical power, for instance an athlete or "muscle man." This corresponds to the anima as Eve. For a woman with such an animus a man is simply a stud; he exists to fertilize the female, to give the woman babies.

In the second stage, analogous to the anima as Helen, the animus possesses initiative and the capacity for planned action. He is behind a woman's desire for independence and a career of her own. A woman with an animus of this type still relates to a man on a collective level, however: he is the generic husband-father, the man around the house whose primary role is to provide shelter and support for his family.

In the next stage, corresponding to the anima as Mary, the animus is the "word," often personified in dreams as a professor or clergyman. A woman with such an animus has a great respect for traditional learning; she is capable of sustained creative work and welcomes the opportunity to exercise her mind. She is able to relate to a man on an individual level, as a lover.

In the fourth stage, the animus is the incarnation of spiritual meaning—a Ghandi or Martin Luther King. On this highest level, like the anima as Sophia, the animus mediates between a woman's conscious mind and the unconscious. In mythology he appears as Hermes, messenger of the gods; in dreams he is a helpful guide. Sexuality for such a woman is more than just an enjoyable physical act; it is imbued with spiritual significance.

Any of these aspects of the animus can and will be projected onto a man, who will be expected to live up to the way the woman sees him—or else. As mentioned earlier, the same is true of the anima. So in any relationship between a man and a woman there are at least four personalities involved. In terms of communication between them, the possibilities are quite bewildering, as shown in the diagram.

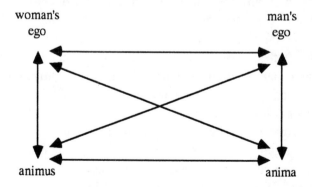

Whenever one partner in an intense relationship is in analysis, they both are. I cannot see Norman in isolation, because he does not exist as a separate person. I can only surmise his wife's psychology from his comments and his experience of her, but if Norman did not fit Nancy like a glove she'd already be long gone—or he would.

It seems to me that Norman's wife's animus hovers between stages two and three. It depends on who she's dealing with. On the one hand she has an image of Norman as husband-father (a role he struggles to live up to); on the other, she has a lover who embodies her own unlived creative life.

In an essay called "Marriage as a Psychological Relationship," Jung speaks of one of the partners as the container and the other as the contained. The contained one lives entirely within the confines of the marriage; there are no essential obligations and no binding interests outside of it. The one who is the container, meanwhile, feels this to be stifling and seeks relief in relationships outside the marriage.[3]

With Norman and Nancy, it is difficult to tell who is container and who is contained: both are having relationships outside the marriage, but at the same time each seeks security, "containment," within it. Clearly they have some work to do on their relationship.

Working on a relationship doesn't mean that partners ought to discuss the psychological meaning or implications of what goes on between them. Far from it. Particularly not when there is a quarrel or ill feeling in the air. It is quite enough to acknowledge that one is in a bad mood or feels hurt, as opposed to psychologizing the situation with talk of anima and animus and complexes and so on. These are after all only theoretical constructs, and focusing on theory is sure to drive one or the other into a frenzy. Relationships thrive on feeling values, not on what is written in books.

You work on a relationship by shutting your mouth when you are ready to explode. By not inflicting your affect on the other person. By quietly leaving the battlefield and tearing your hair out. By asking yourself—not your partner—what complex in you was activated, and to what end. The proper question is not, "Why is he or she doing that to me?" or "Who do they think they are?" but rather, "Why am I

---

[3] See *The Development of Personality,* CW 17.

acting in this way?—Who do *I* think they are?" And more: "What does this say about my psychology? What can I do about it?" That is how you establish a container, a personal temenos.

Instead of accusing the other person—"You're driving me crazy" —you say t ourself, "I feel I'm being driven crazy—where, in me, is that coming from?"

It is true that a strong emotion sometimes needs to be expressed, because it comes not from a complex but from genuine feeling. This is a fine line to recognize, and that's another value in having a container. You can tell the difference if you have something to slosh things around in. And then you can speak from the heart.

Norman's emotions, for instance, don't all come from complexes. Some arise from needs crucial to his individuation. When he can tell the difference, then it will be time to speak.

On the whole, you work on a relationship by keeping your mood to yourself and examining it. You neither bottle up the emotion nor allow it to poison the relationship. The merit in this approach is that it throws us back entirely on our experience of ourselves. It is foolish to imagine we can change the person who seems to be the cause of our heartache. But with the proper container we can change ourselves and our reactions.

It used to be thought that "letting it all hang out" was the thing to do. This is merely letting the complex take over. The trick is to get some distance from the complex, objectify it, take a stand toward it. You can't do this if you identify with it, if you can't tell the difference between yourself and the emotion that grabs you by the throat when a complex is active. And you can't do it without a container.

The endless blather that takes place between two complexed people solves nothing. It is a waste of time and energy and as often as not it actually makes the situation worse. This is a matter of general experience. Jung puts it quite graphically: "When animus and anima meet, the animus draws his sword of power and the anima ejects her poison of illusion and seduction."[4]

---

4 *Aion,* par. 30.

The meeting between anima and animus is not always negative, of course. The two are just as likely to fall in love. But the major battles in relationships happen because the man projects his anima onto the woman and the woman projects her animus onto the man.

We may understand this intellectually, but when someone we love does not behave as we expect—when he or she strays from the image we have of them—all hell breaks loose. That is what it looks like to be complexed. Our emotions do not coincide with what is in our heads. Our reactions run the gamut between blind violence, seething anger, abject disappointment and grieved silence, depending on our psychology. Whatever the immediate reaction, it feels like a piercing of the heart.

Projection that takes place in a therapeutic relationship is called transference. Norman has been seeing me for only a month, and already he has projected—transferred—onto me the image of an authority. I have in effect become a surrogate father. For him I carry all the value that one associates with a wise old man.

This doesn't have much to do with me personally. It was underway even before he came to me. Part of it comes from a cultural expectation of anyone in a so-called healing or helping profession. Part of it is due to Norman's own psychology and the need for meaning in his life. I represent a way to discover that meaning. It is natural for him to confuse me with his own inner healer—to project onto me the knowledge about himself that is actually in him. When that rises to the surface—if it does—he will see me more as I am than as he imagines me to be.

I know this because I have had three analysts who all, for a time, were to me as gods—and one was a goddess. Transference, like any projection, can be thrilling and life-enhancing but has little to do with the other person.

And what about my feelings for Norman, the countertransference? Well . . . let's just say I'm rooting for him.

4

The Hero's Journey

*Every content of the unconscious with which one is not prop-
erly related tends to obsess one for it gets at us from behind. If
you can talk to it you get into relationship with it. You can
either be possessed by a content constellated in the unconscious, or you can have a relationship to it. The more one represses it, the more one is affected by it.*

—Marie-Louise von Franz, *Redemption Motifs in Fairytales.*

*I grant . . . that possibilities exist in me, possibilities close at
hand that I don't yet know of; only to find the way to them!
and when I have found it, to dare!*

—Franz Kafka, *Diaries.*

Norman was out of sorts. He'd had a scene with his wife.

At last, I thought.

"Two things. Nancy asked me where I was when I didn't come
home the other night. I just blew up. I told her it was none of her
business. I was surprised at myself! I'm not that kind of guy. And I
don't think I ever talked to Nancy like that. I mean we never fight.
As it happens I was with an old girlfriend, but it would only hurt her
if she knew."

He grimaced. "Shit, I couldn't get it up anyway."

"Then last night, Nancy told me she was going out. 'Where to?' I
asked. 'To the movies,' she said. 'Who are you going with?' 'A
friend.' 'What kind of friend?' 'Oh you're so suspicious!' she said—
and she took off.

"I put the kids to bed and drank half a bottle of scotch. Then I had
a couple of joints. I really felt awful. She was quite cheerful when
she got back. I apologized for snapping at her. We went to bed and I
cried on her shoulder."

Norman shook his head. "Christ!" he said. "I felt like beating her up and I found myself saying I was sorry! I know she was with him, I just know it!"

He calmed down. "At least she was happy. I can't begrudge her that, can I?"

I asked Norman if he'd had any dreams.

He leafed through his notebook. "Yes, I did. It was last night. There was this horse, a milquetoast man was trying to subdue it. The horse is the man's wife." He looked up. "That's what I wrote." He read again. "It gallops around suburban streets, absolutely wild, it refuses to be handled. He says to it, 'C'mon honey, what's got into you?'

"While I was watching this a man came up, I think it was Martin, he offered me his old leather motorcycle jacket and a pair of boots."

Norman scratched his head. "What do you make of all that?"

"I don't know." I say this quite often, because it's true. "What's your association to horses?"

Norman smiled. "I used to ride horses when I was a kid, oh eight or nine years old. I loved it. They were so free and I was too. I had a happy childhood."

I asked Norman how he felt about his suburban neighborhood.

"It's great!" he said. "It's clean, it's really convenient. The school is close by, playground across the street, shopping center just around the corner. We have some fine neighbors . . ."

He stopped and pursed his lips. "Okay, the truth is I don't like it very much, but we can afford it. I wouldn't be there by choice. You know what, there are no trees there! Everything's concrete."

I wondered aloud about Martin, the man in the dream who offered him boots and a leather jacket.

"Ha!" Norman laughed. "Martin's an old friend, goes back to university days. I love him! He was the quarterback on the football team. I played badminton, I was never much of a sport.

"Martin's a shrewd cookie. Always knew what he wanted. The rest of us didn't have a clue. He's a wheeler-dealer lawyer now, I see him from time to time. He's been married a few times, he doesn't take any shit from women. Martin's the kind of guy you'd trust your life with, he'd never let you down."

Norman became very thoughtful. "As a matter of fact, he's a ruthless son of a bitch. He's really pretty arrogant. I guess you'd call him a jock."

*

That was an interesting session. Norman's shadow is coming into his life. It manifests as self-righteousness. I prefer this to self-pity. I can sit for hours and listen to people feeling sorry for themselves, but enough is enough; after awhile you want to see some action.

Norman doesn't yet see the moral discrepancy between what he is doing and what he expects of his wife, but apparently his body does. If he can't or won't say no, his penis damn well can and will.

Norman sees himself as a civilized man. In his head he grants his wife the freedom to do whatever she wants—whatever makes her happy—but his shadow, which is rather more primitive than Norman is, won't tolerate infidelity. I am glad to see that, it will make for some healthy conflict.

His dream is informative. His wife is out of control. I hear this two ways. On an objective level, his actual wife, Nancy, refuses to behave the way he expects her to, and on a subjective level his inner feminine, his anima, is kicking up the traces. The action takes place in a suburban setting, which from Norman's associations is not congenial to his life-urge, nor, I dare say, to his wife's.

And why is his wife pictured as a horse?

Horse and rider together represent the harmonious movement of energy. The rider is the ego, while the horse is a symbol for animal instincts. In Norman's dream the two are at odds. The writings of Freud have established the fear-significance of horses on the one hand, and the sexual meaning of riding fantasies on the other. (Remember *The Rocking-Horse Winner* by D.H. Lawrence?) Also, and in this context at least as relevant, the horse in mythology has many associations with mother goddesses.[1]

This part of the dream confirms what I already know, that Norman's instinctual life is determined by his mother complex.

The key to the dream—where Norman's energy wants to go—is Martin's offer of his leather jacket and a pair of boots. A jacket, as something put on, an outer covering, refers to a persona. The boots point to an individual standpoint. If the purpose of dreams is to compensate a conscious attitude, then this is a good example.

As a current shadow figure in Norman, Martin fits the bill. Norman would, if he could, deny his feelings to keep the peace, to not rock the boat. Martin, from Norman's associations, is not so inclined. He's a man's man, he'd never put his head in his wife's lap or cry on her shoulder. Norman needs Martin's motorcycle jacket, a tougher persona, and the boots, a new standpoint—particularly when dealing with women. At least then he could say no.

On the other hand, Martin clearly has a problem with relationships, so he is not the be-all and end-all of masculinity.

Martin's characteristics exist in Norman. They're dormant, but if they weren't there he wouldn't have such a dream. To what extent they become an active part of Norman depends on many factors, not least of which is Norman's conscious assessment of what he can live with. The intent of the dream is not to turn Norman into Martin, but to present Norman with an image so different from the way he sees himself that he will seriously consider his conscious attitudes and where he stands.

Whether he stays with his wife or not, Norman is done for unless he can integrate his shadow. And for the time being, because Norman is emotionally too sensitive, his shadow looks much like Martin.

When I first started analysis, shadow was just a word to me—an interesting concept. True, it explained much about human nature that was otherwise quite puzzling. I had read *Dr. Jekyll and Mr. Hyde.* I

---

[1] See Jung, "The Battle for Deliverance from the Mother," *Symbols of Transformation,* CW 5, par. 421n.

had seen *The Secret Life of Walter Mitty*. I knew about the shadow in my head. But I didn't really understand what was meant by the term until I experienced it.

I remember going to a party one evening to celebrate a friend's opening at a prestigious art gallery. It was a posh affair. About two dozen friends of the artist sat down to a banquet at a long table. There were six courses and a vintage wine with each. I was seated opposite a middle-aged woman who talked at me nonstop through the soup. She had an opinion about everything, delivered in a high-pitched grating voice.

Midway through the salad I suddenly stood up and dumped my bowl on her head. Lettuce and tomatoes and chives and cucumbers and an excellent oil and vinegar dressing ran down her hair and dribbled into her lap.

She was shocked, but no more than I. Good God!—I was mortified. It was a very embarrassing situation. Fortunately her husband had a sense of humor, because she didn't.

That very afternoon I had been talking to my analyst about Jung's description of the shadow, specifically the notion that a mild-mannered person must be sitting on a lot of repressed aggression.

"There's no aggression in me," I insisted. "I never get upset about anything."

It was true. I was the perfect gentleman, always polite and accommodating. I could not remember ever being angry at anyone. Oh, occasionally I felt some irritation, but that was well under control. I suggested to my analyst that over the years I must have integrated my shadow very well. He just smiled.

The next time I saw him I was more humble. "I don't know what got into me," I shrugged helplessly.

My analyst chuckled. "It's really quite simple. Your shadow had had enough of her opinions—her animus."

Everything about yourself that you are not conscious of is shadow. Before unconscious contents have been differentiated—recognized as one or another complex—the shadow is in effect the whole of the unconscious.

The shadow is a direct consequence of light. Whatever is illuminated casts a shadow. The higher the sun moves in the sky, the shorter is the shadow—but it has more definition. Light and sun are metaphors for consciousness.

Psychologically, the shadow opposes and compensates the conscious personality. The realization of how and when it enters our life is a precondition for self-knowledge. The more we become conscious of the shadow, the more substantial it becomes—and the less of a threat.

In Jung's description, the shadow—or at least its dark side—is composed of morally inferior wishes and motives, childish fantasies and resentments, etc.—all those things about ourselves we are not proud of and regularly seek to hide from others. In civilized societies aggression is a prominent aspect of the shadow, simply because it is not socially acceptable; it is nipped in the bud in childhood and its expression in adult life is met with heavy sanctions.

By and large, the shadow is a hodge-podge of repressed desires and uncivilized impulses. It is possible to become conscious of these, but in the meantime they are projected onto others. Just as a man may mistake a real woman for the soul-mate he yearns for, so he will see his devils, his shadow, in other men. This is responsible for much acrimony in personal relationships. On a collective level it gives rise to political parties, war and the practice of scapegoating.

Naturally, the realization of the shadow is inhibited by the persona, the ideal image we have of ourselves. The latter is heavily influenced both by what is acceptable to others and, in a culture based on predominantly Christian values, by the Ten Commandments. To the degree that we identify with the bright persona, the shadow is correspondingly dark. The persona aims at perfection. The shadow reduces us to the merely human.

We do many things under the influence of a shadow fed up with the persona. We cheat on expense accounts, we steal, kill and sleep with our neighbor's wife. And then we wonder what came over us.

The first time I stole, at age four, was from my mother's purse. "You can have a couple of pennies," she said. I took three. "Three is not a couple," my mother said with some heat. I pretended I didn't know the difference. The next time was in grade two, when I copped two candies off the teacher's desk. This was discovered and I was sternly admonished in front of the whole class. I think nothing can equal the humiliation you feel when you get a tongue-lashing in front of your friends in grade two—with your mother watching.

I was incorrigible, however. As a trusted teenage employee in a local drugstore, I regularly pocketed chocolate bars. I knew it was wrong, but I couldn't help it. I told myself I did it because I wasn't being paid enough—that was my shadow talking. As a young man my shadow lost his sweet tooth and became more practical, he only stole typewriter ribbons.

When I was living in Zurich I took to wandering around the liquor store, palming price stickers off cheap bottles and tacking them on to expensive wine.

"You're playing a dangerous game," my analyst warned. "The Swiss police have given people twenty-four hours' notice to leave the country for much less serious offences."

"My shadow did it," I laughed. But I stopped, knowing that would be no defense in court.

Responsibility for what the shadow does rests squarely on the ego. That is why the existence of the shadow, once acknowledged, is a moral problem. It is one thing to realize what your shadow looks like—what you are capable of. It is quite something else to determine what you can live out, or with. In practice, this evolves through trial and error.

At the time I am writing this, a top official in a major Canadian institution, a vice-president, has just been fired because on his job application five years ago he lied about his academic background. He claimed he had a graduate degree from a well-known university. A local newspaper, doing a routine story, discovered that this was not true; in fact he had twice failed the final examinations. The man in question, hitherto respected by his peers and said to have had political ambitions, has just been buried by his shadow.

This is happening all the time, everywhere. In hamlets, villages and cities around the world, the unacknowledged shadow is having its say, destroying lives. Often literally.

The conflict between shadow and persona is invariably present in a midlife crisis. Those who do not have such a conflict when they enter analysis soon develop one. It sometimes seems as if they had only been waiting to find someone to trust so they could safely collapse. The characteristic depression at such times indicates the need to realize that one is not all one pretends or wishes to be.

Norman is in his shadow whenever he makes love to a woman other than his wife. He does not experience a conflict over these episodes because he represses their incompatibility with his persona as a devoted husband and family man.

Ironically, the man his wife is having an affair with is really none other than Norman's shadow. He is all that Norman consciously is not. He is an artist, an intuitive feeling type. Norman is a businessman; his talents lie in the realm of thinking and sensation. The other man lives close to his instincts, not particularly concerned about social propriety. Norman lives in his head, caught up in the world of outer appearances.

I begin to see more clearly why Norman is in such anguish: he has an ego-shadow split. It could as well be called a persona-shadow split, since Norman's ego is not substantially different from his persona. Meanwhile, his wife is playing around with his shadow—which Norman doesn't even know exists.

There is no generally effective technique for assimilating the shadow. It is more like diplomacy or statesmanship, and it is always an individual matter. Shadow and ego are like two political parties jockeying for power. If one can speak of a technique at all, it consists solely in an attitude. First one has to accept and take seriously the existence of the shadow. Second, one has to become aware of its qualities and intentions. This happens through conscientious attention to moods, fantasies and impulses. Third, a long process of negotiation is unavoidable.

But the shadow is not only the dark underside of the conscious personality. The kettle we call black is also good for making tea. And so there is a positive side to the shadow. It consists of those aspects of oneself that could be called unlived life—talents and abilities and positive moral qualities that have long been buried or never been conscious. They are potentially available to the personality and their conscious realization often releases a surprising amount of energy.

That is why a person in depression is counseled to go into it rather than escape it. You don't find buried treasure unless you dig.

A midlife crisis constellates both sides of the shadow: those qualities and activities we're not proud of, and new possibilities we never knew were there. Associated with the former is a sense of shame and moral distaste. The latter may have morally neutral connotations, but they are often more frightening because if we follow up on our unknown possibilities there's no telling what might happen.

"Look," I said to my analyst one day when I found myself on the horns of just such a dilemma, "I'm scared. If I take this job I might fall on my face."

He smiled benignly. "The good," he said, quoting Jung, "is the enemy of the better."

"It feels like jumping out of a plane without a parachute," I said, smiling right back.

"Look at it this way," he said, more seriously. "It is quite possible to live with some insecurity."

I said something similar to Norman in one of our sessions. He looked blank. "What do you mean?"

"The positive mother complex," I pointed out, "ties a man to, among other things, the known and the familiar, in other words what he has always felt secure with. For example, he will continue in a certain lifestyle long after it has ceased to feed him simply because he fears what might happen if he stops, which may be exactly what he needs in order to realize his potential."

That was rather more than I usually say. I hate to intrude on what I believe to be a natural process. On the other hand, sometimes a sharp blow to the head doesn't hurt.

"So what should I do?" asked Norman. I swear it was about the tenth time.

"I haven't the foggiest idea," I said, back-pedalling like mad. "Ask the man who owns one," I suggested, pointing at him.

At the time I was thinking of the creative side of Norman's shadow, his unrealized potential. Unacknowledged, the shadow can bring you to grief. Without a moment's notice it can destroy your whole life. Given some attention, it can just as well work the other way: facilitate your extrication from situations that are anathema, and open your eyes to new opportunities.

Norman's initial situation, the underlying problem that took him into analysis, can also be seen in terms of puer psychology.

The expression *puer aeternus* literally means "eternal child." In Greek mythology it designates a child-god who is forever young, like Iacchus, Dionyus, Eros. The theme is immortalized in the modern classics *Peter Pan* and *The Picture of Dorian Gray.*

In the psychology of neurosis the term puer is used to describe an older man whose emotional life has remained at an adolescent level, usually coupled with too great a dependence on the mother. (The term puella is used when referring to a woman, though one also speaks of a woman with a puer animus.) Many midlife crises arise from the inner need to grow out of this stage of development.[2]

The typical puer does not look his age. He is usually quite proud of this, as Norman is. Who wouldn't be, in a culture where youth is valued more than old age? Norman would be shocked at the suggestion that his youthful appearance derives from emotional immaturity. I could point this out to him, but why would I? I prefer to give him time to realize it himself, and if he doesn't, *tant mieux.*

The puer is not responsible for his actions. What he does is not within his conscious control; he is at the mercy of his unconscious.

---

[2] Jung made several passing references to the puer syndrome, but the major study of the subject is Marie-Louse von Franz, *Puer Aeternus: A Psychological Study of the Adult Struggle with the Paradise of Childhood,* 2nd ed. (Santa Monica: Sigo Press, 1981), an interpretation of Saint-Exupéry's *The Little Prince.*

He is especialy vulnerable to his instinctive drives. He is prone to do what "feels right." However, he is so alienated from his true feelings that what feels right one minute often feels wrong the next. Hence he may find himself in erotic situations that cause him a good deal of distress the next day—or indeed that night, in his dreams.

The individuating puer—one who decides to come to grips with his attitudes and behavior patterns—cannot so easily justify what he does by what "feels right." He knows that undifferentiated feelings are highly suspect, especially when they arise in conjunction with the use of alcohol or other drugs. Instead of identifying with his feelings, he tries to keep some distance from them, which means becoming objective about what he is experiencing. He questions himself: Is this what I really feel? Is this what I want? What are the consequences? Can I live with them? Can I live with myself? How does what I do affect others?

The puer has a hard time with commitment. He likes to keep his options open, can't bear to be tied down. This is actually true of Norman, in spite of his strong tie to home and hearth. Or maybe even because of it. While he is professing undying commitment to his family, his shadow is running as fast as he can the other way.

The typical puer acts spontaneously, often to the detriment of himself or others, or both. The individuating puer may have to sacrifice this rather charming trait—but what he sacrifices as a routine way of being then becomes part of his shadow. In order not to become an automaton, completely ruled by habit and routine, he will have to re-assimilate—this time consciously—his former puer characteristics.

In many respects the puer lives a provisional life. There is always the fear of being caught in a situation from which it might not be possible to escape. His lot is seldom what he really wants, he is always "about to" do something about it, to change his lifestyle; one day he will do what is necessary—but not just yet. Plans for the future come to nothing, life slips away in fantasies of what will be, what could be, while no decisive action is ever taken to change the here and now.

I had an aunt who was like that. "One day my ship will come in," she would say, patting my little head as we trotted off to play bingo in the church hall. It never did, perhaps because she lived inland, a thousand miles from the nearest port.

The provisional life is a kind of prison—the death row of the soul. The bars are the parental complexes, unconscious ties to early life, the boundless irresponsibility of the child. The dreams of puers are full of prison imagery: chains, bars, cages, entrapment, bondage. Life itself, existential reality, is experienced as imprisonment. They yearn for independence, they long for freedom, but they are powerless to pull it off.

The writer Franz Kafka was of this type. He explored the symbolism of the prison, and its relevance to himself, about as well as any artist ever has. In one of his enigmatic aphorisms he describes how it feels to be trapped, locked up in his own psyche, with only himself as his keeper. It is the picture of a man who is really free to come and go as he pleases, but unable to make a move:

> He could have resigned himself to a prison. To end as a prisoner—that could be a life's ambition. But it was a barred cage that he was in. Calmly and insolently, as if at home, the din of the world streamed out and in through the bars, the prisoner was really free, he could take in everything, nothing that went on outside escaped him, he could simply have left the cage, the bars were yards apart, he was not even a prisoner.[3]

The prison is a symbol familiar to the analyst as a refusal of the individuation process. This is symptomatic of the psychology of the puer, who chafes at boundaries and limits and tends to view any restriction as intolerable. Psychologically, however, some restrictions are indispensable for growth. This is expressed in the I Ching, the Chinese book of wisdom, as follows:

---

[3] "He," in *The Great Wall of China and Other Pieces,* trans. Willa and Edwin Muir (London: Secker and Warburg, 1946), p. 134. The symbolism of the prison in puer psychology, with particular reference to Kafka, is explored at more length in my book *The Secret Raven: Conflict and Transformation* (Toronto: Inner City Books, 1980), pp. 68ff.

Unlimited possibilities are not suited to man; if they existed, his life would only dissolve in the boundless. To become strong, a man's life needs the limitations ordained by duty and voluntarily accepted. The individual attains significance as a free spirit only by surrounding himself with these limitations and by determining for himself what his duty is.[4]

Marie-Louise von Franz describes the prison phobia of a mother-bound man and interprets it:

The prison is the negative symbol of the mother complex . . . or it would be prospectively just exactly what he needs, for he needs to be put into prison, into the prison of reality. But if he runs away from the prison of reality, he is in the prison of his mother complex, so it is prison anyway, wherever he turns. He has only the choice of two prisons, either that of his neurosis or that of his reality; thus, he is caught between the devil and the deep blue sea. That is his fate, and that is the fate of the *puer aeternus* altogether. It is up to him which he prefers: that of his mother complex and his neurosis, or that of being caught in the just-so story of earthly reality.[5]

It is a lucky puer—like Norman—whose unconscious eventually rebels and makes its dissatisfaction apparent through a midlife crisis. Otherwise you stay stuck.

The puer's shadow is the senex (Latin for old man)—disciplined, controlled, conscientious, ordered. The shadow of the senex is likewise the puer—unbounded instinct, disordered, intoxicating, whimsical. The puer has much in common with the Greek god Dionysus, whose frenzied female followers ripped men to pieces. Senex psychology is characterized more by Saturn and the god Apollo—staid, rational, responsible.

Both puer and senex, Dionysus and Apollo, have their place. But whoever lives out one pattern to the exclusion of the other risks constellating the opposite. A healthy, well-balanced personality is capable of functioning in a Dionysian or Apollonian way, according to

---

[4] Hexagram 60, "Limitation," in *The I Ching or Book of Changes*, trans. Richard Wilhelm (London: Routledge & Kegan Paul, 1968).

[5] Von Franz, *Puer Aeternus*, p. 137.

what is appropriate. That is the ideal, seldom achieved without a good deal of conscious effort. Hence a midlife crisis quite as often involves the need for a well-controlled person to get closer to the spontaneous, instinctual life as it does the puer's need to grow up.

Where does Norman fit into all this? Well, he has at least one foot in the puer camp. His other foot is somewhere out in space, looking for a shoe, an appropriate standpoint.

Personally, I am a lapsed puer. Just like a reformed smoker or alcoholic, I tend to be impatient with those still caught in this syndrome. At the same time, if I can get past my distaste for what I've been, it's possible for me to empathize with their situation. Norman is a good example. There is virtually nothing he's done that I haven't, none of his attitudes that I don't recognize in myself. In fact, in unguarded moments I can even get nostalgic about it.

Norman doesn't yet realize it, but on the day he walked into my office he embarked on a heroic adventure.

It is a hero's task to do something out of the ordinary. For Norman this means trying to understand why he acts and reacts the way he does. His life takes on the flavor of a fairy tale. There is a wicked witch (his mother complex) to overcome or outwit, and there are helpful animals (his instincts) to see him through the night. Also, like the dummling in many fairy tales, he is quite naive. This actually works in his favor: just like in fairy stories, many of the "tasks" he will be required to carry out will only be possible if he suspends his rational way of looking at things.

The hero's goal is to find the treasure, the princess, the golden egg. Psychologically these all come to the same thing: himself—his true feelings, his unique potential. You either win the princess or you stay in the basement, there's no in between.

Mythologically, Norman is caught up in a time-honored tradition. Among other things, the hero's way involves a night sea journey, a motif represented by imprisonment or crucifixion, dismemberment or abduction, etc.—the kind of experience weathered by sun-gods and heroes since time immemorial: Gilgamesh, Osiris, Christ, Dante,

Odysseus, Aeneas and many others (including Pinocchio). In the language of the mystics it is called the dark night of the soul.

The hero's journey is a round; the pattern is well known, as illustrated in the diagram below.[6]

Typically, in myth and legend, the hero journeys by ship, fights the sea monster, is swallowed, struggles against being bitten or crushed to death, and having arrived inside the belly of the whale, like Jonah, seeks the vital organ and cuts it off, thereby enabling his release.

CALL TO ADVENTURE

All the night sea journey myths derive from the perceived behavior of the sun, which, in Jung's lyrical image, "sails over the sea like an immortal god who every evening is immersed in the maternal waters and is born anew in the morning."[7] The sun going down, analogous

---

[6] Adapted from Joseph Campbell, *Hero with a Thousand Faces*, Bollingen Series XVII (Princeton: Princeton University Press, 1949), p. 245.

[7] *Symbols of Transformation*, CW 5, par. 306.

to the loss of energy in a depression, is thus the necessary prelude to rebirth. Cleansed in the healing waters, the ego lives again. Or, in another image, it rises from the ashes, like the phoenix.

Psychologically, the whale-dragon is the mother. The battles and the suffering that take place during the night sea journey symbolize the heroic attempt to free consciousness from the deadly grip of the mother, the unconscious. The vital organ that must be severed is the umbilical cord. The potential result is the release of energy—the rising of the sun on a new day—that has been tied up with the shadow and other unconscious contents.

Norman did not choose the hero's journey. It chose him. He would avoid it if he could. Who would willingly leave the comfort of home to face dragons? Who would give up television and popcorn in front of the fire for a whale's belly? But something in Norman demands the journey and he is obliged to live it out whether he likes it or not.

I cannot save him from the hazards he will face, nor would I even try. What nature has ordained, let no man interfere with.

Norman is gripped by an inner imperative that must be allowed to run its course. The most I can do is sit with him and alert him to some of the dangers.

5

Reality As We Know It

The four functions are somewhat like the four points of the compass; they are just as arbitrary and just as indispensable. Nothing prevents our shifting the cardinal points as many degrees as we like in one direction or the other, or giving them different names. . . . But one thing I must confess: I would not for anything dispense with this compass on my psychological voyages of discovery.

—C. G. Jung, *Psychological Types.*

Norman was late for his appointment. He came in breathless, seventeen minutes past the hour. I scowled because I don't like to be kept waiting.

"I'm sorry," he said, "but I couldn't help it."

"You could have phoned," I said. I really felt grumpy.

"I was trapped in the subway," said Norman. "A guy threw himself off the platform in front of a train." He shrugged. "What could I do? The whole system ground to a halt."

I softened. These things happen. I just wish they didn't.

Norman settled in and brought up a new topic. "I've been reading Jung's typology," he said.

"Reading it or reading about it?" I asked.

I'm conservative, a purist when it comes to Jung. Others may go beyond him, mine the same mother lode and emerge with gems that to them are more sparkling, but I'm still trying to reach his bootstraps. Arnold, the friend I lived with in Zurich for a few months, feels the same way. It could be called an unresolved transference. Arnold calls it the power to constellate.

"I have a contract with this company in Syracuse," said Norman. "I was down there this week, talking to their personnel manager. She

told me they don't hire anybody without giving them a type test. I
picked one up."

He rummaged in his briefcase. "Here it is," he said, pulling out a
pamphlet. "'Applying the Myers-Briggs Type Indicator to Increase
Productivity and Organizational Effectiveness.' According to this it's
based on the work of Carl Jung." Norman looked at me. "I didn't
know he had made it into the business world."

I frowned. "Jung's typology did—he didn't."

My feeling for Jung makes me ambivalent toward current type
tests. Although they're based on Jung's model, they lack its subtlety.
It's true they can be helpful but they can also be misleading. They
can give a reasonable picture of the way one functions at the time of
the test, but since they do not account for the dynamic nature of the
psyche they say nothing about who took it—the ego? the persona?
the shadow? some other complex?—or the possibility of change.
Type tests weren't what Jung had in mind when he spent eight years
writing *Psychological Types.*

In the struggle to understand yourself, there is no substitute for
prolonged self-reflection.[1]

Norman was leafing through the pamphlet. "It looks interesting.
Why is it important?"

"That's a feeling-type question—what's it worth to you? Well, I'll
tell you. Everything psychic is relative. It's like Einstein's theory of
relativity in physics and just as significant. You can't say, think or do
anything that isn't colored by your particular way of seeing the
world. That's your typology.

"People are different. That seems obvious, but it's easy to forget.
Everyone has strengths and weaknesses. Jung's typology is a way of
putting these differences into some order. It's helpful in understanding yourself and it's a godsend in relationships. If you realize
that someone functions in a particular way, you can make al-
lowances. You can compensate for your personal disposition and

---

[1] I have written about this, and much more, in *Personality Types: Jung's
Model of Typology* (Toronto: Inner City Books, 1987).

welcome those who function differently. Maybe you
something yourself. Maybe, in a given situation, a different way of
functioning would be more appropriate."

I was breathless. The teacher comes over me sometimes.

"I don't like the idea of labeling people," said Norman.

"Neither do I, neither did Jung. In fact he specifically warned
against it. That's misusing the model. It's a tool for psychological
orientation, just as a compass is used to determine where you are in
the physical world.

"Here's Jung's basic model," I said. I took a pad and did a quick
sketch. "There are four functions—thinking, feeling, intuition and
sensation. The first two and the last two are opposites. Then there's
introversion and extraversion—each of the four functions can work
in an introverted or an extraverted way.

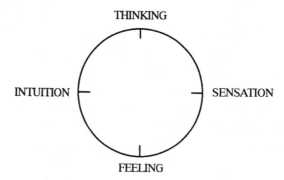

"You can turn the circle any way you like. I just arbitrarily put
thinking at the top; any of the others might be there, depending on
which function a person favors most."

"Don't go too fast," said Norman, taking notes.

"The sensation function is concerned with tangible reality, the
physical senses; it establishes that something exists. Thinking tells us
what it is. Feeling tells us what it's worth to us, and through intuition—which Jung described as perception via the unconscious—we
have a sense of what can be done with it."

"That's too fast," said Norman.

"Sensation excels at details, it takes things in like a photographic plate; intuition doesn't—it's more interested in possibilities. The thinking function is concerned with ideas, and feeling focuses on relationship."

I went to my bookcase. "Listen to this." I opened *Psychological Types* and read:

> For complete orientation all four functions should contribute equally: thinking should facilitate cognition and judgment, feeling should tell us how and to what extent a thing is important or unimportant for us, sensation should convey concrete reality to us through seeing, hearing, tasting, etc., and intuition should enable us to divine the hidden possibilities in the background, since these too belong to the complete picture of a given situation.[2]

I closed the book. "The ideal is to have conscious access to the function appropriate for a particular situation."

"Neat," said Norman, "is that possible?"

"Maybe not. In practice, one function is usually more developed than the others. It's called the primary or superior function."

"Superior, meaning better?"

"No. One function isn't any 'better' than any other; superior means the one you're most likely to use."

"What happens to the others, the ones that aren't developed?"

I smiled. "They give you a hard time. They get you from behind. They pop out unexpectedly. Especially the inferior function, the one you're least good at. It's always the one opposite to the superior function. A one-sided emphasis on thinking, for instance, is always accompanied by an inferiority of feeling, and a well-differentiated sensation function shuts out intuition. And vice versa, of course."

"Does typology have anything to do with what you call my midlife crisis?" asked Norman.

"I was coming to that," I said. "Part of the problem leading up to a breakdown is that some of the functions have been neglected; they

---

2 *Psychological Types,* CW 6, par. 900.

finally demand to be recognized. That's painful. It's usual then to project the cause of the pain onto somebody else.

"But in fact it's aspects of yourself wanting to be recognized and accepted. Remember, anything you usually aren't is shadow. That includes the inferior function. A breakdown is a golden opportunity, really, because there's a lot of energy tied up with the inferior function. Making it conscious often brings a new lease on life."

I could write another book on this, but I focused on Norman.

"Can you have two good functions?" he asked.

"Yes, one of the functions that isn't opposite to the primary function is often quite well developed. For example, thinking goes well with sensation or intuition; a superior sensation function can have feeling or thinking as a good secondary function, and so on."

I drew another sketch. "Then you have something that looks like this—intuition and thinking work together in the speculative thinker; thinking and sensation combine for empirical thinking, etc."

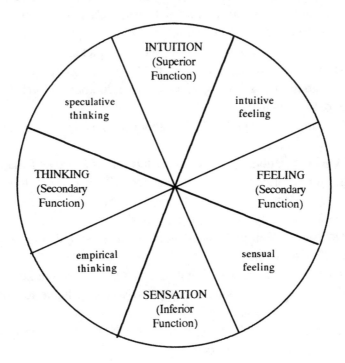

Norman studied my drawing. "How do you know what your best function is, and which one's inferior?"

"It's not easy," I said, "because when you get into a complex all the functions are distorted by emotion. We don't see straight, we can't think, when we're angry; even happiness colors the way we feel about things and people; we can't properly evaluate what something is worth to us when we're upset; and possibilities dry up when we're depressed. You can be sure you're functioning well below par when you're complexed."

"Now I'm completely confused," said Norman.

Good, I thought. Confusion is the beginning of wisdom.

"Using Jung's model in your life is a matter of watching yourself," I said.

"How do you mean?" asked Norman.

"As you move through the world you ask yourself, 'In this situation, or with that person, how did I function? With what effect? Did my actions and the way I expressed myself truly reflect my judgments—that's thinking and feeling—and my perceptions—sensation and intuition? And if not, why not? What complexes were activated in me? To what end? How and why did I mess things up? What does this say about my psychology? What can I do about it? What do I *want* to do about it?'"

Norman was thoughtful. "What about introversion and extraversion?" he said.

"A good question. They are completely different ways of adapting to the world. The introvert is hesitant and reflective, the extravert is open and outgoing, loves meeting new people." I considered. "That's an oversimplification, you really should read Jung."

"Do you think an understanding of typology would help me and Nancy?" said Norman.

I nodded. "Perhaps. Jack Spratt and all that. You might keep it in mind in terms of your kids, too. Otherwise you're liable to expect things they aren't capable of."

Norman got his things together to leave. "Do you have friends who never heard of Jung's typology?"

"Yes, of course."

"How do you stand it?"

I shrugged. "I play poker with them. And win."

He tucked a copy of my book on types into his briefcase. At the door he paused. "So what type do you think I am?" he asked.

I expected this. Norman wants to save himself some work.

"I don't know. The functions aren't really differentiated in you. You're still a bowl of soup."

He flinched.

"Don't take it personally." I shook his hand. "Most people are."

*

Alone that night, my mind went back to the time with Arnold in Zurich. I learned almost as much about typology from living with him as I did from reading Jung.

Arnold was a raving intuitive. I met him at the station when he arrived. It was the third train I'd met. True to his type, his letter wasn't specific. True to mine, I was.

"I've rented a house in the country," I told him, hefting his bag. The lock was broken and the straps were gone. One wheel was missing. "Twelve and a half minutes on the train and it's never late. The house has green shutters and polka-dot wallpaper. The landlady is a sweetheart, we can furnish it the way we want."

"Great," said Arnold, holding a newspaper over his head. It was pouring out. He had no hat and he'd forgotten to bring his raincoat. He was wearing slippers, for god's sake. We couldn't find his trunk because he'd booked it through to Lucerne.

"Lucerne, Zurich, it's all Switzerland to me," he said philosophically.

It was quite amusing at first. At that time we didn't know each other very well. I didn't know what was in store. I'd never been close to anyone quite so . . . well, so *different*.

Time meant nothing to Arnold. He missed trains, he missed appointments. He was always late for class, and when he finally found the right room he didn't have anything to write with. He either had bags of money or none at all, because he didn't budget. He didn't know east from west, he got lost whenever he left the house. And sometimes in it.

"You need a seeing-eye dog," I joked.

"Not as long as you're around," he grinned.

He left the stove on overnight. He never turned out lights. Pots boiled over, meat turned black, while he sat on the porch watching the sky. The kitchen was forever filled with the smell of burnt toast. He lost his keys, his wallet, his lecture notes, his passport. He never had a clean shirt. In his old leather jacket, baggy jeans and two different socks he looked like a bum.

His room was always a mess, like a hurricane had hit.

"It drives me crazy just to look at you," I hummed, adjusting my tie in the mirror.

I liked to be neatly turned out, it made me feel good. I knew precisely where everything was. My desk was ordered, my room was always tidy. I turned out the lights when I left the house and I had an excellent sense of direction. I didn't lose anything and I was always on time. I could cook and I could sew. I knew exactly how much money was in my pocket. Nothing escaped me, I remembered all the details.

"You don't live in the real world," I observed, as Arnold set out to fry an egg. A real hero's journey. He couldn't find the frying pan and when he did he put it on the wrong burner.

"Reality as *you* know it," he said, quite hurt. "Damn!" he cursed. He'd burnt himself again.

I need not say much here about the added aggravations due to Arnold being an extravert and me an introvert. Enough to say there were plenty. He brought people home at all hours of the day and night. I liked privacy, my own quiet space. I was concerned to keep to my timetable. During the day I escaped to my room and studied, or pretended to. At night I lay in bed with a pillow over my head, listening to them carouse.

On the other hand, Arnold's way of functioning was sometimes quite helpful. Like when we furnished the house.

Our landlady Gretchen, a trim and efficient Swiss business-woman, gave us a free hand. She had taken a fancy to Arnold. God knows why, he didn't present as well as I did. "Just pick out what you want," she said. "You do the shopping, I'll pay the bills."

I had a few things in mind. So did Arnold. My ideas were quite modest, Arnold's were not. We already had beds and a few chairs. "A nice comfortable sofa," I said, as we entered the department store. "A bookcase and a desk for each of us, a couple of lamps. That's all we need."

"You have no imagination," said Arnold, steering me to the antiques. "You do the talking."

Naturally. I had not come to Switzerland without learning some German. Before leaving Canada I took a Berlitz course for six months. I wasn't fluent but I could make myself understood. I could also get by in French. Arnold knew no French and could not even count in German. I think he did not realize he was coming to a foreign country. I scolded him about this more than once.

"A few phrases," I implored. "Try saying hello, *Guten Tag.*"

He shrugged. "They all speak English."

As it turned out, they didn't. Worse, and to my chagrin, the language of the streets was Swiss German, a dialect, almost as different from German as Welsh or Scottish is from English. I was just about as helpless as Arnold.

Back to the department store. In one language or another, we managed to spend a lot of our landlady's money. While I fumbled to say exactly what I meant, Arnold waved his hands and gesticulated. By the time we left, ushered out by a grateful crowd of salespeople, we had a few things I hadn't thought of: a Chinese screen, two Indian carpets, a complete set of dishes, eight pounds of bratwurst and several numbered prints by Miro and Chagall.

Gretchen was thrilled. She gave us a special dinner. Arnold stayed behind when I left. "I'll just wrap up the lease," he grinned.

I struggled to appreciate Arnold. I wanted to. His outgoing nature, his natural ebullience, were charming. I admired his air of careless confidence. He was the life of every party. He easily adapted to new situations. He was a lot more adventurous than I was. Everywhere we went he made friends. And then brought them home.

He had an uncanny sense of perception. Whenever I got in a rut, bogged down in routine, he had something new to suggest. His mind was fertile; it seethed with plans and new ideas. His hunches were usually right. It was like he had a sixth sense, while I was restricted to the usual five. My vision was mundane—where I saw a "thing" or a "person," Arnold saw its soul.

But problems constantly arose between us. When he expressed an intention to do something I took him at his word. I believed he meant what he said, that he would do what he announced he was going to. This was particularly annoying whenever he failed to turn up at a certain time and place. It happened quite often.

"Look," I'd say, "I counted on you being there. I bought the tickets. Where were you?"

"I got waylaid," he'd counter defensively, "something else turned up, I couldn't resist."

"You're unstable, I can't depend on you. You're superficial and you're flighty. Why, you don't have a standpoint at all."

That isn't how Arnold saw it.

"I only express possibilities," he said, when for about the tenth time I accused him of being irresponsible, or at least misleading me. "They aren't real until I say them, and when I do they take on some shape. But that doesn't mean I'll follow up on them. Something better might occur to me. I'm not tied to what I say. I can't help it if you take everything so literally."

He went on: "Intuitions are like birds circling in my head. They come and they go. I may not go with them, I never know, but I need time to authenticate their flight."

One morning I got up to find yet another pot boiled empty on a hot burner. Arnold struggled out of bed, looking for his glasses.

"Have you seen my razor?" he called.

"God damn it!" I shouted, furious, grabbing an oven mitt, "one day you'll burn down the house, we'll both be cinders. 'Alas,' they'll say, scooping our remains into little jars to send back to our loved ones, 'they had such potential. Too bad one of them was such a klutz!' "

Arnold shuffled into the kitchen as I threw the pot out the door.

"Oh yeah?" he said. "You made dinner last night for Cynthia, I wasn't even here."

It was true. My face got red. My balloon had been pricked. Reality as I knew it just got bigger.

"I'm sorry," I said meekly. "I forgot."

Arnold clapped his hands and danced around the room. "Join the human race!" he sang. As usual, he couldn't hold a note.

It was not until then that I realized Arnold was my shadow. This was a new revelation. It shouldn't have been—we had already established that our complexes were radically different—but it did, it struck me like a thunderbolt. I said as much to Arnold.

"Never mind," he said. "You're my shadow as well. That's why you drive me up the wall."

We embraced. I think that incident saved our relationship.

All that was a long time ago. In the intervening years I've become more like Arnold. And he, indeed, more like me. He can tell left from right now, and he actually learned to crochet. His attention to detail is often sharper than mine. He lives alone and has a magnificent garden. He knows the names of all the flowers, in Latin.

Meanwhile, I have dinner parties and sometimes I haunt the bars till dawn. I misplace precious papers. I forget names and telephone numbers. I can no longer find my way around a strange city. I pursue possibilities while things pile up around me. If I didn't have a cleaning lady I'd soon be overwhelmed by dirt.

Such developments are the unexpected consequences of getting to know your shadow and including it in your life. Once this process is underway it's difficult to stop. You can never go back to what you were, but what you lose on the roundabouts you make up on the swings. You lose something of what you've been, but you add a dimension that wasn't there before. Where you were one-sided, you find a balance. You learn to appreciate those who function differently and you develop a new attitude toward yourself.

I see Arnold from time to time. We are still shadow brothers, but now the tables are somewhat turned.

I tell him about my latest escapade. He shakes his head. "You damn gadabout," he says, punching my shoulder.

Arnold describes quiet evenings by the fire with a few intimate friends and says he never wants to travel again. This man, this great oaf, who as I used to know him would be off and running at the drop of a hat.

"You're dull and predictable," I remark, cuffing him.

*

"I like it," said Rachel. "It's rich."

Rachel is my anima. We don't always see eye to eye, but on the whole she's a helpful muse. I talk to her from time to time, to keep me on track.

"Do you think I was too hard on Arnold?" I asked. "I wouldn't want to hurt his feelings."

Rachel laughed. "A little hyperbole never hurt anyone," she said. "That's your mother complex talking."

Rachel's usually right.

6

Toujours Grimace

Which is harder: to be executed, or to suffer that prolonged agony which consists in being trampled to death by geese?

—Kierkegaard, *Journals.*

"Look," said Norman, "I remember what you said about the puer. I do want to grow up. But I'd like to be able to be a kid when I feel like it. Do I have to lose that?"

"I don't know," I said.

It is typical of the puer to think in terms of either/or, this or that, black or white. Living in the gray zone, holding the tension between opposites, does not come easy to the puer.

"Anyway, I've stopped smoking grass." He pulled out his notebook. "Listen to this dream. I'm lost in a desert, sitting on the sand. The sun is beating down, it's hotter'n hell. I've about given up hope. Suddenly there's music in the air and way in the distance, over the dunes, comes a marching band.

"When they get closer I see it's a bunch of dwarfs with drums and trumpets and trombones. They sing and do somersaults. They're carrying a huge sign that reads: STOP SMOKING DOPE."

We had a good laugh at that. It wasn't the first dream he'd had of being in a desert. He knew it to be not just a lifeless place but traditionally where you come to grips with devils and experience some kind of revelation. I told him that dwarfs in dreams are like helpful animals in fairy tales. Music is associated symbolically with feeling, the function that tells us what something is worth to us. I was glad to see it constellated in Norman.

"I'm not saying I won't smoke again," he said. "I've had a lot of fun with grass. I'm a different person when I'm stoned. My cares disappear. The world opens up, I feel free as a bird."

105

Of course, I thought. It releases his shadow.

"But I'm interested to see what happens without it."

Norman was silent for a long time. When this happens I know something is looming. People in analysis are seldom silent because they have nothing to say. After all, they are paying a hefty wack to speak their mind. When they say nothing, it's usually because they're thinking of how to express what's going on inside. I've had analysands who said nothing for the whole hour, for weeks at a time. And when the torrent came, I didn't get a word in for a month.

In my early years as an analyst I was not comfortable with silence. The clock ticked away. Time is money; they weren't getting their money's worth. I maintained a placid front but inside I panicked. I should say something to start them going, give them a helping hand. Arnold said that was my positive mother complex getting me. I think he was right.

Now, in the midst of teeming silence, I watch the rainbows on my walls. They come from the sunlight passing through the beveled glass in the windows. That's on sunny days. When it's cloudy I pick lint off my pants. True, I still pass the kleenex to wipe away the tears, but I say nothing.

When Norman finally spoke, it was a portentous statement.

"I've decided to be celibate," he said, crossing his legs. "Well, monogamous."

I maintained a bland exterior, but inwardly I clapped my hands. Give up dope and stop screwing around, at one fell swoop!

I inclined my head. "You'll miss a lot of fun," I ventured.

Norman wasn't taken in. "You're testing me," he said. "But I've been thinking about it for weeks. I'm sure it's the way to go. Nancy's still seeing her . . . her friend"—he almost choked on the word—"but that's up to her. I know what's right for me. I have this gut feeling. Unless I commit myself to one relationship, I'm lost.

"I'm thinking of putting it to her: mutual fidelity, we don't have other lovers, we try to make a go of it between us. If her friend is more important to her than our relationship, then I'll leave. What do you think of that?"

I observed that his mother complex might give him a rough time.

"You like harmony," I said. "If your wife is not ready for this hard stand—and she still thinks you don't know she has a lover—she'll be mad. What'll you do then? She may be very attached to this other man. She may depend on him for her survival. What if she doesn't want to give him up? How will you deal with that? What will you do if she chooses him over you? What if she laughs at you? *What about the Terrible Mother?"*

I got quite excited and didn't try to hide it.

Norman stayed calm. He'd come some way in three months.

"Well, I had a dream. It was after I went to a party. There was this pretty little wisp, Wendy, she thought I was really something. I said a few words and she was enthralled. The juices were running, I can tell you. I wanted to say yes, it felt just fine, but I went away for awhile and thought about it."

He was very serious. "I sat in the kitchen and counted up all the women I've had since I've been married. I lost count at thirty-five." He blushed. "I mean Je-suz! I screwed everything in sight! Some of them were crazy as loons and I didn't notice! I don't even remember half their names! And why? Because I wasn't happy at home, that's why. And I always felt guilty about it. I'm surrounded by guilt, it's like living in a bowl of jelly.

"I told Wendy I liked her but I was married. I said no!"

And used your wife as your first line of defense, I noted.

"What was your dream?" I said.

"I went to bed in a good mood," said Norman. "I made a few tentative overtures toward Nancy. She didn't respond, but it didn't seem to bother me. I lay there and fell asleep feeling great.

"I dreamed my mother phoned. She was in a house and burglars were trying to get in. 'I need you,' she said. She wanted me to come and rescue her. I told her I was too busy and hung up. I woke up feeling really excited."

We sat for awhile in silence. Saying no to a woman was for Norman equivalent to taking a stand against his mother complex. We both knew that. In several previous dreams Norman had busted his ass to save his mother. I remembered his initial dream, where he was in a burning building with his mother. In a later dream, he rushed into a blazing house and carried her out on his back; in another, he actually cut off his genitals and handed them to her—just like Attis in the Greek myth, the son-lover who castrated himself in the service of his jealous mother Cybele. We did not need to speak of these dreams. They hovered between us.

I don't know what was going on in Norman, but I was thinking of Jung's remark that what was required for a man to grow up was "a faithless Eros, one capable of forgetting his mother and undergoing the pain of relinquishing the first love of his life."[1]

I sighed, remembering the day I picked up the phone to call my mother and couldn't remember her number.

"You have changed," I said. "Perhaps your wife has not."

"I don't know," mused Norman. He looked directly at me. His eyes were luminous. "I know I don't want to go on as we have, as if everything's okay with me. I just don't want to pretend anymore. Yes, she may not like it. I may not be able to stand it myself. I don't know. I guess I'll just have to deal with the consequences."

*

I was very proud of Norman. I didn't say this to him because if I did he might bask in my appreciation. Inflation is always a danger. Much better, I thought, to leave him on the hook for awhile, see what happens.

He had worked up some momentum. I didn't know what it would lead to, but my fingers were crossed. "Never halt on a shifting slope," writes René Daumal, "The mountain is always watching for a chance to give you a spill."[2] I thought of all those would-be fairy tale heroes who didn't make it up the glass mountain.

---

[1] *Aion,* CW 9ii, par. 22.

[2] *Mount Analogue: An Authentic Narrative,* trans. Roger Shattuck (London: Vincent Stuart, 1959), p. 105.

After Norman left I took out my old journals, now musty and yellow. I hadn't looked at them in years. They start when I went into analysis twenty years ago and finish five years later, soon after I left Zurich. I found them in a box behind the furnace. I was surprised I hadn't gotten rid of them long ago.

It was a painful business, reading that stuff. Dreams, snatches of poetry, trivial accounts of the daily grind. I wept. I gnashed my teeth. I wanted to throw up. I could hardly believe what I'd been. Page after page of pain and self-pity. It was a shameful chronicle of the puer, barely relieved by flashes of insight.

How did I ever get my Diploma?

And when I did, what did it mean?

Then I went through my old "creative" writing. The same old crap, only worse. There was a raft of short stories and three novels, all unpublished—the kind of material famous writers in later life refer to as juvenilia. There was very little to be proud of. No wonder I got so many rejection slips. I read a few, bemused. Most were form letters. One was puzzled but gracious:

> It is hard to know what to make of your material. Your manuscript is a strange hybrid—philosophy grafted onto a slight fictional framework. On the positive side, many passages are quite beautiful, and the whole work has a certain poignant dignity. . . .

I remember saving that one because I liked the phrase "poignant dignity." That was almost as good as getting published. I met the editor who wrote it, a woman, a few years later at the Frankfurt Book Fair. She didn't remember me. Now she has her own publishing house and lives just down the street. I have a fantasy of one day dropping into her office and chewing the fat as equals.

I had a stiff drink and chewed another Rolaid. I mentally measured myself against Norman. In almost every way he was ahead of where I had been in his shoes. At his stage of analysis I was still blaming my wife for everything. His latest decision, to commit himself to one relationship, was something I never even thought of until about six months later. And his realization that taking a stand involved consequences he would have to deal with . . . well, I still have trouble with that.

And the way Norman looked at me. He usually avoids my eyes. Today he looked directly at me, no evasion. I have to respect that. The eyes are the windows of the soul. When you look into someone's eyes, it's as if you hold their psyche in the palm of your hand. I think I was more than two years into analysis before I dared expose myself like that.

I went to bed feeling very depressed. I was not fit to be an analyst. I was a fraud. I might as well be reading tea leaves. I could not be any help to anyone. There was certainly nothing about me to inspire confidence in the so-called individuation process.

That's what you call negative inflation—identifying with the things you don't like about yourself.

It was a long time since I'd recorded a dream. But that night I did.

I was in a university lecture theater, giving a talk to a class of first year students. "And that's what life's all about," I concluded jauntily, tossing the chalk in the air. I had my eye on a young co-ed about half-way back. She was really cute.

A boy in the first row stood up. He was maybe nineteen. "Isn't it true," he said, "that you left your family?" He looked around him and snickered. The audience murmured.

"I did."

"You abandoned your wife and kids?"

I hung my head. "I did."

"You left them *penniless?"*

"Wait, you don't understand . . . I had no choice . . ."

The young snot took a whip from his waistband and was about to lash me when Jung himself appeared, stage right.

"Stop!" shouted Jung. He was old, at least eighty. He stooped and had a cane. He hobbled between me and the students. "This man is human," he said, pointing to me. "That is his only crime." He turned to face me and said, "Go, leave this place. Do your work and stop feeling guilty."

I woke up feeling rather better.

*

The next time Norman came he was in bad shape. He slouched into my office with his old hang-dog look.

You poor schmuck, I thought, she's got you by the balls.

"I'm destroyed," he said, sinking into a leather wing-chair.

I waited.

"It was awful," said Norman. "She bit me. Oh, not literally. Nancy is too much the lady for that. Her way is more subtle. She can put the boots to me and not leave a mark."

He grimaced.

"I'd been in Buffalo for the day. I went to sew up a major contract. I could have stayed overnight and hung around the bar. There are lots of possibilities in bars. You never know what might turn up. Did I ever tell you about Sheila and her trained monkey? They were quite a pair. We had a nice thing going until she started phoning me at home and sending baskets of grapes. I told Nancy it was a case of mistaken identity."

Because Norman has a well-developed sensation function, his intuition, which perceives possibilities, is colored by his shadow— morally suspect, a little less than ethical.

"I resisted the temptation to stay and play. I came home. I was really looking forward to being with Nancy and the kids. That's normal for me, of course, I almost always get homesick when I'm on the road. But often I've stayed away just for the possibility of some excitement. You know how it is—you have a long day, you have a few drinks and you want a warm place to put it. I could never count on Nancy being available, if you know what I mean. Like I said, she wouldn't refuse me, but it's no fun partying on your own."

Get to the point, Norman, I've heard this before.

"Nancy always makes a nice dinner when she knows I'm coming home. She's a gourmet cook, she took classes for three years. I was looking forward to a good meal, a pepper steak, say, rubbed in garlic—Nancy makes an incredible sauce béarnaise—and a nice bottle of wine—I like a vintage Beaujolais-Villages, '84 and '85 are good years. We'd play awhile with the kids, put them to bed and have a quiet chat by the fire. A real homey atmosphere, your typical happy family. Just like it says in the ads, right? I'd put on some music—the Beatles, maybe, we've always liked them, or the McGarrigle sisters, or maybe Sting, fantastic lyrics, he's in Jungian analysis in England, did you know that?"

This kind of meandering detail drives me crazy. I want the facts, thunk! thunk! thunk! Norman's discourse is like a snake weaving through the weeds. He'll get to where he's going, eventually, but meanwhile he savors the journey. I shouldn't begrudge him that, straight lines aren't always the most direct. I feigned calm.

". . . and it all went wrong," Norman was saying.

"It all went wrong," I nodded, knowingly.

"In the first place, we didn't have steak, we had fish. It was sole meunière, poached to perfection of course, but I don't happen to like fish. It makes me gag because I'm always looking for the bones.

"Secondly, Nancy forgot to get some wine. All we had was apple juice. I hate apple juice. It reminds me of worms.

"Then the kids. I mean I love my kids, I really do. But they're just impossible, who can be with kids and keep sane? Ian will only eat cereal or Kraft dinner. Nancy says this is a phase that will pass but I'm not so sure. He sat there patting his corn flakes, one by one, getting them all under the milk. He won't eat toast either unless it's buttered right to the edge. I thought I would scream. Jennifer still wets her pants and refuses to blow her nose. Her cheeks are like leather from rubbing in all the snot."

I began to laugh. It's that or cry. Norman caught the mood.

"They can't sit still without watching television and they refuse to do jigsaw puzzles. Tiddley winks! Lego! Old Maid! Cabbage Patch dolls! Transformers! Electric trains! They have them all, they won't even look at them. They can't read and they can't fucking write!"

We both collapsed, gasping.

Norman recovered.

"I put the kids to bed while Nancy soaked in a hot bath. I thought that was a good sign. She's usually more open to making love after a bath. I undressed and put on my dressing-gown, the one she gave me for Christmas. I tiptoed down to the living-room and set the scene. I put on a record, *Frank Sinatra's Greatest Hits,* she loves him. I got out the Grand Marnier and two balloon glasses and lay on the rug in front of the fire.

"Okay, I thought, this is it. I'll put it to her straight. True confessions. I'll admit to a few affairs—not the neighbors, nothing too close to home—and tell her I know all about her and Boris. I'll swear off other women and pledge my undying love. She'll do the same, and in the fading light from dying embers we'll make crazy love. Bogart and Bacall. Just like in the movies."

Norman looked at his feet. "When Nancy came down she was all dressed up, fresh make-up and everything. 'I'm going out for awhile,' she said. I couldn't hide my disappointment. My jaw fell about two feet. 'It's 10.30,' I said, 'are you sure this trip is necessary?'

"Nancy was putting things in her purse. 'It's Valerie's opening tonight, I thought I told you. I promised her I'd go.'

"Valerie is this wierd friend of Nancy's who does pottery. It's quite fancy stuff, some people call it art. When Valerie drops in she bounces off the walls. Even the cats run and hide. I don't like Valerie and I don't like her pots.

" 'I was thinking we'd have a talk,' I said. I ran my finger around the rim of my glass so it went whoo-whoo.

" 'And what were you thinking of talking about?' said Nancy, just a shade sarcastic.

"I felt pretty silly by then, lying on the floor half naked, but I plunged on.

" 'We could start with Boris,' I said.

" 'Boris? What about Boris?' She folded her arms. Nancy always folds her arms when she feels vulnerable.

" 'Is he going to the opening?'

" 'He might be there,' said Nancy. She wouldn't meet my eyes. 'You're welcome to come.'

" 'Sure, and spoil your fun,' I said miserably.

" 'You're pathetic!' said Nancy. I cringed, she's never attacked me before. We've weathered some silent hostility but I've never seen her like this.

" 'You're not here half the time and when you're home you expect me to drop everything. You think I don't know what you're up to when you're away? You think I don't know where all those grapes came from? Do you think I'm stupid? Well I'm fed up! Life goes on, you know, it doesn't depend on you. I'm not playing solitaire when you're away and I'm damned if I will when you're here!'

"I couldn't speak. My tongue was stuck to the roof of my mouth. I just stared at her and bit my lip.

" 'Don't wait up,' she said as she left."

Norman sank back in the chair and closed his eyes. Somewhere the birds were singing, but here we were in Mudville.

"I was crushed. I had a joint and finished the Grand Marnier. I paced around for awhile, thinking of where I'd rather be. I finally went to bed. Nancy crawled in beside me about three o'clock. I cuddled up to her, spoons. She didn't turn to greet me, but she didn't wince either. I think, yes, she even gave me a little help when I bundled it in from behind. We haven't made love for weeks. It just felt so good to be inside her again."

*

So Norman is back at square one, in thrall to the mother, his wife. He was about to win the brass ring, pin the tail on the donkey, and what does he do? The first chance he gets, he crawls back into the womb. Thankful it's still there to receive him.

I don't blame him for that. God knows I've been there, writhing in the sheets. But I'm not responsible for Norman. He can make it or not. I absolutely refuse to mother him. He's on his own, sink or swim. It's not my problem.

Then why do I feel like I've been drawn and quartered?

I think of a comment by Rilke, in *The Notebooks of Malte Laurids Brigge:* "I have no conception of the amount of succor that is constantly being used up."[3] And my facetious imitation in a book I wrote: "What a lot of succor there is, and what an enormous drain it all runs into!"

Okay, I had high hopes for Norman. He could have been a contender. I got both feet in, I lost my objectivity. I mistook bravado for integration. Perhaps, at this point in the twentieth century, it is too expensive to be a Romantic. Even Nietzsche would have to have a paper route to survive today.

Alas, poor Norman, I knew him well. A man can't change himself by reason, or sheer force of will; he can only become what he potentially is. And even when change does take place, the old ways continue to exert a powerful attraction. As Jung writes,

> Whoever sunders himself from the mother longs to get back to the mother. This longing can easily turn into a consuming passion which threatens all that has been won. The mother then appears on the one hand as the supreme goal, and on the other as the most frightful danger—the "Terrible Mother."[4]

Bye-bye Norman. I saw it coming but I expected too much. There are no guarantees in this process. He just didn't have what it takes. Mentally I am getting ready for the next analysand.

But wait, this session is not over.

*

Norman opened his eyes. "I had a dream that night. A nightmare, actually. There's an iron belt around my middle. A big man—god he's a giant!—is pulling both ends of the belt. It's so painful, I can hardly breathe. I think I'll be cut in two if he doesn't let up. It's mortal combat. I get hold of a sledgehammer and hit him, again and again, right between the eyes. I am appalled at this violence, it's not like me at all. I woke up in a panic."

---

[3] *The Notebooks of Malte Laurids Brigge,* trans. John Linton (London: The Hogarth Press, 1959), p. 200.

[4] *Symbols of Transformation,* CW 5, pars. 351f.

I'm alert now, tuned in.

Cutting through the middle is related to the imagery of crucifixion, with overtones of dismemberment. Both symbolize the suffering involved in differentiating the opposites and learning to live with them. They are integral to the hero's journey. Jung writes about it:

> Nobody who finds himself on the road to wholeness can escape that characteristic suspension which is the meaning of crucifixion. For he will infallibly run into things that thwart and "cross" him: first, the thing he has no wish to be (the shadow); second, the thing he is not (the "other," the individual reality of the "You"); and third, his psychic non-ego (the collective unconscious).[5]

Norman still has little understanding of his shadow and certainly no wish to be it; the "other" is his wife, whose reality escapes him; and the psychic non-ego, the unconscious, is what got him into this in the first place.

The giant has been here before. It represents the enormous affect associated with a complex. In Norman's case, it is a stand-in for the mother. In other dreams, giants have chased Norman up trees and into sewers. Once a giant ate his foot. This is the first time he's actually fought back.

"Congratulations," I said.

I don't think he heard me. Just as well. It may have happened in the dream, in compensation, because he couldn't do it in reality.

"The next day was really heavy," said Norman. "I woke up with a splitting headache. There was frost on the window. I took a good look at myself in the mirror. I'm getting hairs in my nose."

Holy Toledo, I thought, it's enough to drive me back to Beckett.

"I had nothing pressing so I took the day off. Nancy was still sleeping. The dining-room table was littered with debris from the night before. I hate mess, I wished it gone. The kids woke up in high spirits, noisy. I used to wear earplugs but I can tell you they don't really help.

---

[5] "The Psychology of the Transference," in *The Practice of Psychotherapy,* CW 16, par. 470.

"I cleaned up and made the kids some porridge. I had orange juice myself. Nancy doesn't like it when I skip breakfast. 'You need something hot in the morning,' she says. I often feel the same, but porridge isn't the answer.

"I walked the kids to school and on the way back I dropped in to see Linda. She's a model, we sometimes play bridge with her and her husband."

Norman sighed. "She was interested and I wanted to, but again, I couldn't get it up."

He was still. I leaned forward so as not to miss a word.

"By the time Nancy got out of bed I was out back, fixing the garage door. She's been after me for weeks to do something about it. The hinges weren't in the right place, it didn't close properly. It was not an easy job, but I did it.

"Nancy didn't speak all morning. I passed her often enough, getting tools, but she never said a word. I didn't either because I was afraid to. You don't cross Nancy when she's in a mood."

Norman paused, then went on.

"I have this fantasy about a happy family, or so it seems until one day the husband goes off for a loaf of bread and never comes back. . . . No signs beforehand of any mental upset. No history of instability. On the contrary, he has always been very placid, the neighbors speak highly of him, he even helps with the dishes. And then one day he runs screaming from the house. . . . Or appears on the roof of a ten-story building, say, threatening to jump, or holes up with an arsenal in a restaurant, picking off patrons. . . .

"By noon I was fit to be tied. I was desperate to speak to her. She was working in the garden in her wooden sandals. That's a very safe place for Nancy, I guess it's a kind of temenos for her. There are some flower borders and a small vegetable patch. Last year I put in some marijuana plants, they grew higher than the corn. I'm not very fond of gardening myself, but I dig the earth up every fall and spring because Nancy says nothing will grow if you don't prepare the ground.

"I went down to the basement and had a joint. After a time I felt like a warrior. I went out to see her with a trowel. I would joust my way into her heart."

I rolled a cigarette. This is where it gets sticky.

"I took a magazine with the latest horoscope column. Nancy and I took a night course in astrology a few years ago, did I tell you? I do the charts and she interprets them. She's quite intuitive. Nancy's a Gemini, I'm a Taurus."

Air and earth, they don't mix. There is some interesting symbolism in astrology, but it was no help to me when I was on my knees.

"At first I played it cool," said Norman. "I sat beside her and pulled out some weeds. I actually find this quite restful. It's the planting I don't like, putting seeds in is hard work.

" 'Any odd jobs I can do for you?' I said.

"Nancy jabbed at the ground and didn't look at me.

" 'Here, listen to this,' I said, picking up the magazine: 'Though your ruling planet protects you from the slings and arrows this month, take no unfair chances—beware of emotional tension. You may get your own way but it gives you no real pleasure, especially if it involves those younger than yourself.'

"This struck me as significant because Nancy is a few days older than me. There was another line: 'The 28th is a favorable time for gains.' I didn't read that out loud because it was the 28th.

"Nancy took a piece of kleenex from her sleeve and wiped her nose. 'You're making that up,' she said.

" 'I'm not,' I said, handing it over, 'see for yourself.'

"The sun caught her hair. There's an aristocratic look about Nancy. High cheek-bones, fine-spun hair, smooth skin. She's quite pretty, actually, and I do love her.

" 'Did you see yours?' said Nancy, reading: 'Unforeseen changes in your way of life are likely either at the beginning or the end of the month. Domestic harmony could be upset for awhile but things take a decisive turn before long. Travel is indicated in the meantime, bringing pleasure.'

"She looked sideways at me. 'Now couldn't that mean a holiday? We haven't been away for months. Valerie just came back from Maine. She says it's God's country, there are lots of really nice camping grounds.'

"I have always resisted holidays with my family. I'm sorry about that, but they never seem to work out. You take more stuff than you need and everything you want is back at home. Hotels were not made for small children, all they want to do is jump on the beds and punch the buttons in the elevators.

"In the early years, I let myself be talked into camping. Nancy loves nature, the out-of-doors. So do the kids, for about ten minutes. Did you ever try to sleep in a tent when it's raining and you forgot to put up the fly sheet? Or when it's 90 degrees and the mosquitoes find the holes in the netting? Did you ever wake up at five in the morning, still pitch-dark, with a herd of cows chewing your clothes?

"A full-grown cow is nothing to mess with. Nancy knows exactly how I feel about camping.

"I held up my hands. 'Truce,' I said. 'There's something I have to say.'

"Nancy took off her gardening gloves and sat back on the grass. She had no make-up on and her hair was in a bun. She looked pretty bleak. My heart went out to her. I didn't want to make her feel bad. I could buy her a new dress, take her to the opera, give her a treat—a pound of cashews, say, a box of Turtles. But I pressed on.

" 'I don't like you seeing Boris.'

"I said it as gently as I could, considering. 'Okay, I've been with other women but I'll stop. I think that's our only chance. I want an honest relationship.'

"Nancy looked at the trees, her brow knit. 'You're stoned again.'

" 'I had a small toke,' I said defensively.

" 'One day you'll get arrested,' she said. 'Have you no feeling for me at all?'

"I was taken aback. 'What do you mean? I love you. I just can't live with you like this.'

"Nancy clenched her teeth. 'I don't like it any more than you do,' she said. 'Do you have to make me feel guilty?' Her eyes filled with tears. 'What about the children?'

"I felt awful. I know that Nancy's greatest fear is to be left alone with the kids. I think she's never recovered from her father leaving. I feel sorry about that but it's not my fault. I held my ground.

" 'I can't take it anymore,' I said. 'I can just about cope with you not wanting to make love to me. But when you do it with somebody else, it's too much.'

"Well, that set her off. She denied that Boris was anything but a friend. She lectured me on being suspicious, the evil effects of jealousy. 'It's a real sickness in you. All I have are my friends. Is that too much to ask?'

"The tears flowed. Out poured the bitterness and accusations: my affairs, her loneliness and silent suffering, her guilt and anguish. Recriminations, resentment, animosity. How cold and unloving I am, how heartless and rigid, my absolute lack of compassion. How unreasonable I am, how unfeeling. If I really loved her I would understand her needs, etc. and etc. They were heavy guns. I only had a trowel.

"Then she got real calm. 'There's another thing,' said Nancy. 'When it comes to making love, you're still ham-fisted. You haven't learned a thing. You're an animal. You're just too damn coarse. I like some refinement. I would think you'd know that by now!' She stamped her foot and turned away. 'I don't know what to do about you, I'm at my wit's end.'

"I wilted, I fell apart. I lost it all. I put my head down and fled to the basement. I felt like a real shit."

Norman sat back and covered his face. "What will I do? There's no place for me."

This lament stung me. I try to be objective but I'm not made of stone. I put my arm around Norman and said everything would work out.

"It's a healthy clearing of the air. With your feelings now out in the open, anything is possible."

I didn't believe it, but that's what I said. As an analyst you sometimes say things you don't believe. In a funny kind of way, it keeps you honest.

7

The Middle of Nowhere

"It makes me breathless," said Rachel. "What happens next? Where do you go from here? I can't wait!"

She was on the sofa. Her legs were tucked under her, a yoga position she finds quite comfortable. Personally, I don't.

"I'm not sure," I said. "He who meets the dragon and hightails it to the basement is no hero. I might leave him there for awhile. Maybe that's where he belongs."

"I thought he showed some real spirit," said Rachel. "He did try. He's had a setback, that's all."

"Maybe so, but it's getting pretty close to home. My intention was to illustrate a midlife crisis, not have another one."

"I like the dialogue," said Rachel. "That scene in the garden is priceless! Is that how it actually happened?"

I squirmed in my wing-chair. "I took some liberties with the facts. Bits and pieces from the past. But it's close to how Norman felt at the time, and true to the way I understand it psychologically."

Rachel mused. "Nancy is not as honest as Norman. Why doesn't she admit to her affair?"

"As I mentioned earlier, she has as much invested in her life with Norman as he has with her. She doesn't want to risk losing it. Of course Norman already knows, but he can't confront her like a man because he's hog-tied by his mother complex."

"Still," said Rachel, "I find her quite a sympathetic character compared to Norman. His antics are pretty extreme. One minute he's a charming Don Juan, sword flashing, the next he's a clown, and then he's a fool. How can a woman live with that? Why didn't Nancy leave him long ago?"

"You have to read between the lines. Maybe I left too much out. In chapter three, where I talk about the animus? I meant to imply that

Nancy has a projection on Norman, something to do with the father; she wants to see him as a genuinely responsible family man. He can't live up to this image because he's too much the puer. But he's a good hook for it. Nancy still has faith in Norman, she keeps hoping.

"Remember, she has no experience of her actual father after an early age. That's very significant. She has no on-going, balanced animus-model that would let her move on psychologically, be more tolerant of men, accept Norman as he is. The void in her experience of the personal father is filled with fantasy—expectations derived from the archetypal father. Norman's role in her life is to make that fantasy real. Strictly speaking, Nancy doesn't even have a father complex; she has a direct line to the father archetype."

"That would make for a formidable animus," observed Rachel.

"Yes, a real heavyweight. Norman didn't have a chance. Goliath won this time."

I liked that line. Rachel didn't seem to notice.

"I'm afraid Nancy's no more conscious of what they're caught in than he is," I said, "and no more able to break out. She's like the spinning woman in those fairy tales, a mother figure whose imagination spurs the hero on to find the treasure. Right there, of course, she's hooked, she *is* the mother.

"That's something I'd like to say more about—the effect of a projection on the person receiving it. The way I see it, Norman would like nothing better than to be the man Nancy thinks he is, or would like him to be. That comes from identifying with her and her needs. It works the other way too: Nancy identifies with the mother because that's what *he* needs."

"It all sounds so complicated," said Rachel. "They keep passing in the night."

"Yes," I nodded. "It's hard to say whether Nancy's expectations of Norman are unrealistic or just premature. I mean maybe he's just not old enough yet. Who knows, he might move gracefully into the senex, once he's had his fill of the puer.

"Of course that's all speculation," I said. "The real tragedy is in the moment. Because of her tie to the father, Nancy's a little girl at heart. She can't respond to Norman sexually because he's still identified in her mind with the idea of father. I imagine she believes that if he were to live up to her notion of what a man is, she'd really go for him—but I don't think so. The incest taboo will never let her respond to Norman as long as she holds on to the image of him as father. She can live with him as a brother, perhaps as her very best friend, but not as a lover."

"What about the incest taboo in Norman?" protested Rachel. "If he has such a powerful mother projection on Nancy, how come he's often impotent with other women but not with her?"

Rachel keeps me on my toes. It didn't seem to fit the theory and I didn't know why.

"Well," I said, "it's historically true—that's the way it was at the time. He could screw her until the cows came home, no problem. I'm not sure about the psychology. I'll have to think about it."

Rachel was leafing through the manuscript. "I'm not sure this part works," she said, yawning. "Where you talk about your old journals and writing? What does that have to do with Norman?"

I couldn't answer that. I had something in mind but I forget what. It didn't seem out of place to me, but I couldn't explain it.

"What's this reference to Nietzsche?" said Rachel. "I don't see the relevance of Rilke's comment about succor. The Kierkegaard thing on geese is quite delightful, but who's René Daumal?"

"They're my old heroes," I said. "Maybe they aren't strictly relevant, but they found their way in. That counts for something. Synchronicity?"

Rachel smiled gamely, but I could see she was fading. She didn't usually stay this long.

"Norman has been living in a world of make-believe," I said. "He thought the work on himself had done the trick. Having at last become able to reveal his true feelings, he'd simply express them and his wife would swoon in his arms. That's what led up to the scene in the garden. He had it all together in his mind. It just didn't occur to him that her reality was different. He doesn't see her any more than she sees him.

"He was due for a fall. It's a regression, the basement is my metaphor for the unconscious. Did you get that?"

Rachel didn't answer. She was almost gone. I brought the session to a close.

"There's nothing unusual about Norman and Nancy. Once they had a good fit, and now they don't. The problem is what to do about it. I suppose the bottom line is that they both have potential, sexual and otherwise, that they can't realize with each other. For a long time I thought they could make it together. Norman thought so too, or he wouldn't have tried."

I put away my notes and shut down the computer. I had more to say about all this, but tomorrow.

8

The Transcendent Function

*The opus consists of three parts: insight, endurance, and action.
Psychology is needed only in the first part, but in the second and
third parts moral strength plays the predominant role.*

—C.G. Jung, *Letters.*

*He is thirsty, and is cut off from a spring by a mere clump of
bushes. But he is divided against himself: one part overlooks the
whole, sees that he is standing here and that the spring is just
beside him; but another part notices nothing, has at most a
divination that the first part sees all. But as he notices nothing he
cannot drink.*

—Franz Kafka, "He," in *The Great Wall of China.*

Norman did not quickly recover. He was shocked. His confidence of
recent months was gone. I could hardly believe it. He slipped back
into a full-blown depression. The knot returned to his stomach. And
to mine.

"Don't think of it as a failure," I said, more cheerfully than I felt.
"A minor regression, that's all, an example of *reculer pour mieux
sauter,* as Jung says—a step back, the better to spring ahead."

Norman looked skeptical.

He made an attempt to explain to his wife how he felt.

"I hurt all over. I have no peace of mind. I feel like a little boy,
lost in the woods."

"You're a grown man," said Nancy, "You shouldn't feel that
way." And then—rather cruelly I thought: "I'm not your mother."

Norman did not try again.

We didn't have many laughs in the next few sessions. Norman
kept his appointments but his spirit was shot. His mood was black. I
longed for some information from the unconscious, a few helpful

127

hints on how to proceed, but he stopped paying attention to his dreams. For long periods he just stared at the wall and sighed. He didn't even notice the rainbows.

"Norman," I said, "Pull yourself together."

"My longing for something real with Nancy was foolish," he said. "I was mistaken, I am only what you see."

"And what about what's inside, longing for life? What about your possibilities?"

"It's okay, I'll be alright. I'll soldier on."

Norman's fear of his wife at that time dominated him completely. He became doubly dependent and would not speak a word against her. He accepted her view of him. "She's right," he said, "I'm an animal. I should be locked up."

"You're 'nothing but' an animal?"

"That's the way it feels."

"You remind me of an entry in Kafka's *Diaries,*" I said. I read it to him:

> At a certain point in self-knowledge, when other circumstances favoring self-scrutiny are present, it will invariably follow that you find yourself execrable. . . . You will see that you are a rat's nest of miserable dissimulations.[1]

"Sound familiar? Try this":

> At bottom I am an incapable, ignorant person who if he had not been compelled to go to school would be fit only to crouch in a kennel, to leap out when food is offered him and to leap back when he has swallowed it.[2]

Norman smiled wanly. "Yeah, that's me."

I became quite worried. I was afraid of what Jung calls the regressive restoration of the persona, which sometimes happens when there's been a major collapse in the conscious attitude. This doesn't

---

[1] *The Diaries of Franz Kafka, 1914-1923,* trans. Martin Greenburg, ed. Max Brod (London: Secker & Warburg, 1949), p. 114.

[2] *The Diaries of Franz Kafka, 1910-1913,* trans. Joseph Kresh, ed. Max Brod (London: Secker & Warburg, 1948), p. 308.

occur only in analysis. Jung gives the example of a businessman who takes too great a risk and goes bankrupt:

> If he does not allow himself to be discouraged by this depressing experience, but, undismayed, keeps his former daring, perhaps with a little salutary caution added, his wound will be healed without permanent injury. But if, on the other hand, he goes to pieces, abjures all further risks, and laboriously tries to patch up his social reputation within the confines of a much more limited personality, doing inferior work with the mentality of a scared child, in a post far below him, then, technically speaking, he will have restored his persona in a regressive way. He will as a result of his fright have slipped back to an earlier phase of his personality; he will have demeaned himself, pretending that he is as he was *before* the crucial experience . . . . Formerly perhaps he wanted more than he could accomplish; now he does not even dare to attempt what he has it in him to do.[3]

Likewise, Norman's experience could smash him completely, or at least cripple him for good.

In fact, being crippled, unable to function in one's usual way, is an apt metaphor for those in a midlife crisis. A person with a broken spirit is in effect crippled. People go into analysis "on their knees." They want to get "back on their feet." A person who has exhausted the superior function "limps along."

In history and mythology, the motif of the cripple is everywhere. There is the lame Hephaestus, blacksmith to the gods; the fisher king in the Grail Legend; a string of wounded Mesopotamian kings; the devil Pan with a goat's foot; Osiris who lost his penis; Harpocrates, son of Isis and Osiris; Mani, the founder of Manichaeism; the Egyptian god Bes, and so on. Being crippled is often a sign of chthonic (earthy) wisdom, as in legends of dwarfs and dactyls, and the Cabiri, sons of Hephaestus.

On the whole, crippledom is associated with heroes and those with an unusual fate. So it was not Norman's being crippled that bothered me, but the possibility that it might have no issue.

---

[3] *Two Essays,* CW 7, par. 253.

It finally came to the point where our relationship was on the line. The self-pity got too thick for me. One day I suggested to Norman that perhaps he'd like to stop seeing me for awhile.

"I can't digest anything any more," he replied, "but don't let that trouble you. I feel very well indeed."

The self-mockery irritated me.

"Or maybe you should see someone else."

"Kick me when I'm down," he said bitterly. "I have no one else."

"This is getting on my nerves. You slouch in and you slouch out. You don't read, you don't keep your dreams and you don't have much to say. There's no edge. There's nothing to get our teeth into. I can't help you if you won't help yourself."

"You would drop me? Just like that?"

"I'm not here to hold your hand. *I'm* not your mother either."

I bit my tongue but the words were out. They hung between us like Banquo's ghost.

Norman closed his eyes and was silent. I didn't mean to go so far. Rachel, I thought, was that you?

I went to the kitchen to refill our glasses. Three ice cubes for Norman, four for me. I splashed water on my face and hung about. Is this how it ends? I thought. With a snivel? Is there no future for Norman?

My mind went back to our first session. I saw something in Norman then. I remembered what I wrote: "Norman is a timely reminder of what I was and the process through which I became a Jungian analyst." What have I missed? I thought. What hasn't Norman done yet that I did?

I racked my brain.

When I returned to the living-room Norman was browsing in my bookshelf, smoking a cigarette. Norman had stopped smoking a few weeks ago because Nancy said it made her ill. "You smell like ashes," she'd said. Brrrr!

This small token of defiance gave me hope.

"What's this about?" he asked. He held up John Sanford's *The Invisible Partners.*[4] He read the subtitle: "How the Male and Female in Each of Us Affects Our Relationships."

"It's about what you're going through now," I said.

Norman sat down and squared his shoulders. "Okay, I'll give it another go. What do you suggest?"

I rubbed my hands. It was coming back.

"Did you ever paint?" I asked Norman.

"Not since grade two," he said. My stomach lurched. "I wouldn't know where to start," said Norman.

I suggested he get some coloring tools and draw or paint when he was feeling low or in a bad mood.

The next session Norman was apologetic. "I tried," he said, "but I'm terrified by a blank piece of paper."

I empathized with Norman because I had had the same kind of block. A friend advised me.

"Try this," he said. "Take a page of a newspaper. It's not empty, not scary. Lay a plate on it. Draw an outline of the plate with a crayon or a colored pencil or a paint brush. Look at what you made. Think about it. Now do something inside the circle. You can do anything you want—squiggles, faces, triangles, squares—anything. It's up to you, do whatever comes."

Norman had more success the next time. He showed me his first efforts with some trepidation.

"These are quite wonderful," I enthused, genuinely pleased.

"What do they mean?" asked Norman.

"I don't know."

The object of this kind of activity, which Jung called active imagination, is to give a voice to sides of the personality that one is ordinarily not aware of—to establish a line of communication between consciousness and the unconscious. It is not necessary to interpret drawings, to figure out what they "mean." You do them and you live with them. Something goes on between you and what you create. It

---

4 New York: The Paulist Press, 1980.

doesn't need to be put into words to be effective. Sometimes articulating it even interferes with the process.

As far as I'm concerned, it's magic.

After I separated from my wife I lived in a basement apartment. It was tiny, a bed-sittingroom and a bathroom. It was very depressing and I cried a lot.

I took my friend's advice and soon the walls were covered with my drawings. I graduated from newspaper to cardboard to good quality bond. I used whatever came to hand: pencils, pen, paint, felt-tipped markers, fingers. My drawings and paintings were crude depictions of whatever was going on in me when I did them. I certainly didn't think of them as art. They had no style or technique and when I look at them now they seem quite grotesque. People who came to visit looked at me with suspicion. But I loved them and my soul rejoiced.

Active imagination can be painting or music, dance or working in clay—whatever you feel like doing. You follow the energy where it wants to go. The less formal training you have the better, because the trained mind inhibits freedom of expression. It is a way of giving the unconscious an outlet, so you don't explode. It is also another kind of container; instead of dumping your affect on other people you keep it to yourself, you take responsibility for what's yours.

Writing too is a form of active imagination. You have a dialogue with what's going on inside. You conjure up an image, personify it and talk to it. Like my chats with Rachel. You write it down—to make it real, give it substance. That's the difference between active imagination and a daydream. If you don't fix it in time and space, it's pie in the sky.

For those in analysis, active imagination of one kind or another is good preparation for leaving. You don't stay in analysis forever. When the time comes to stop it's nice to have some tools to take with you.

Once Norman started painting and drawing, he stopped feeling sorry for himself. He also stopped thinking about what his wife might be doing when he wasn't around. He focused on himself and how he felt. Whenever he got into a mood, he captured it with a concrete image or had a talk with his anima. He stopped imagining that his wife was responsible for his heart-ache; instead, he asked his heart why it ached.

One of Norman's first sketches showed a woman tied to a rock—the feminine fused with matter (mother-bound). Psychologically this relates to the Eve stage of anima development. Norman described it as his "mountain-anima," because it reminded him of fairy tales where the princess is imprisoned on top of a mountain.

"She's a real sweetie," I observed. "But she has no feet."

Norman nodded. "My feelings aren't grounded."

An early painting was a classic image of depression. It showed a man with head bent, under a black cloud. A bird fluttered above him.

"What kind of bird is that?" I asked.

Norman considered. "A raven comes to mind."

In alchemy the raven is a symbol for the *nigredo*—"melancholia, 'a black blacker than black,' night, an affliction of the soul, confusion, etc,"[5]—in short, a state of depression.

---

[5] C.G. Jung, *Mysterium Coniunctionis,* CW 14, par. 741.

I thought of another mournful passage in Kafka's *Diaries.* I found
it and showed it to Norman:

> I don't believe people exist whose inner plight resembles mine; still,
> it is possible for me to imagine such people—but that the secret
> raven forever flaps about their heads as it does about mine, even to
> imagine that is impossible.[6]

"It's the 'poor me' syndrome," said Norman. Again he was im-
pressed to find his feelings so well expressed.

"Yes," I agreed, "heavily laced with inflation, the unconscious
feeling of being special—'Nobody suffers as much as I do.' "

Norman looked sheepish. "As if depression played favorites."

Over the next few months Norman got this stuff out where he
could see it. Then he worked on it. When he came home from a trip
he played with his kids, tucked them in and went to the basement. He
didn't hang around his wife, waiting for a bone. True, he still went to
the basement, but not for a toke. That was his private space, the only
place in the house he could be alone. That was his temenos, where
he communed with himself.

Every time he came to see me, he brought something new. A
couple of drawings, a page or two of inner dialogue, a dream he'd
amplified, a book he'd read.

Once he came with a pair of clay penises. One was tiny, a shriv-
eled little thing; the other was erect and powerful. We set them up
between us.

"Bud Abbott and Lou Costello?" said Norman.

"David and Goliath?" I suggested.

The change in Norman was quite remarkable. His mood light-
ened. His sense of humor returned. Even his appearance altered. He
kept his moustache but he shaved off his beard. He acquired a leather
jacket. Instead of Hush Puppies he now wore black leather boots.

"I'm playing with a new persona," he said, quite pleased with
himself. As if I were blind.

---

[6] *The Diaries of Franz Kafka, 1914-1923,* trans. Martin Greenburg, ed. Max
Brod (London: Secker & Warburg, 1949), p. 195.

In fact I saw in these changes not only a new persona but an outer reflection of Norman's shadow. Slowly he was assimilating his other side—they were coming together.

I know this had something to do with me, but not much. To my mind, the work he did on himself was more valuable than anything that took place between us one hour a week. I put a word in now and then, I made a few observations and I suggested things to read. But Norman, or something in him, was now in control. I was an interested bystander.

The nature of the transference changed. Norman no longer expected me to provide him with answers. He still asked questions, but now they were more often rhetorical, as if he were talking to himself. His inner analyst was constellated. We discussed things man to man; not exactly as peers, but more like brothers than father and son.

One thing that cropped up as part of Norman's shadow was homosexuality. I was not surprised; in a man with a strong positive mother complex, it's the other pole to the Don Juan. As you leave one behind, you come closer to the other.

Norman brought several dreams where he was sexually involved with a robust man, and he had vivid fantasies. These both excited and worried him. He fussed about it.

"Am I gay?" he said. "Have I just been hiding in the closet?"

"I don't know," I said. "Are you actively attracted to men? Do you want to make love to one?"

Norman frowned. "I'm not keen. Do I have to?"

I told him that dreams and fantasies of this kind were quite common. I'd had them myself.

"Look at it symbolically," I said. "That man is your shadow, he wants to get closer. It's up to you whether you act it out or not. You decide."

Through all this, the grip of the mother complex loosened. This became apparent in a new attitude toward his wife.

"I had a dream the other night," he said, reading from his notebook. "I'm in a tower on the top of a mountain. I hear a story about a prince and princess, how they loved each other and then had a lovers' quarrel—a useless quarrel, as it turned out, for they went on to live happily ever after."

Oh-oh, I thought.

Norman smiled ruefully. "I put this to the test. I woke up about midnight with that dream, feeling quite loving. I'd gone to bed early. Nancy was still up, puttering around the kitchen. I coaxed her into bed. She was not unwilling, I thought. I lit a candle and started making love to her.

"There was no response. She wouldn't even kiss me. I went on until she said, very quietly, 'I'd rather not.'

"I left her there and went to the kitchen. I made a ham sandwich and thought about it. You know what? I would have pushed it, but I couldn't get an erection."

Right. I was grateful to Norman for this information. The son-lover is only really potent with the mother. That's what he lives for, to give her satisfaction. That's why Norman has often been sexually ineffective with other women. Take away the mother and it's a whole new ball-game.

"I'm not getting what I need from this woman," said Norman.

He said it like a revelation. It was not news to me.

"For the past two months Nancy has not made a single affectionate gesture toward me. Only sometimes she has been friendlier than at others.

"I went to the basement and got out my colored pencils. I was frustrated and mad. I worked away for about two hours." He handed me a piece of paper. "This is what I did. I made a photocopy for you. That's me, and that's Nancy. What do you see?"

I was stunned. Norman and his wife were joined together at the hip, like Siamese twins, but he was about to step into a barge. His boots were enormous—bigger than his wife's. I saw this as a solid standpoint. The animosity between them was clear: he had a gun pointed at her, and she was armed with a knife. The raven was still there—Norman wasn't out of the woods yet—but the mother, represented by one grotesque breast, was shown spouting nonsense.

"Blah, blah, blah," it said.

It seemed to me to presage a separation. I didn't say this because if it came from me Norman wouldn't have to take the responsibility. He might even be tempted to tell his wife that I'd suggested it. That would be using Dad to manipulate Mom. He had to fight his own battles. I was merely an aide-de-camp.

Besides, it might have symbolized an impending psychological separation, not a physical one. As if to say that Norman and Nancy had lived in each other's pockets long enough.

"It's interesting," I said. "You have a distinctive technique."

*

A few weeks later Norman bounced into my office, full of life. These extraverts, I thought, remembering life with Arnold. They always surprise me.

"I'm leaving Nancy," Norman announced.

I thought of his drawing. It would be a painful break, major surgery.

"What about your kids?" I said. I felt like the little Dutch boy, putting a finger in the dyke. I had to try, but I didn't expect it would hold. Water seeks its own level, willy-nilly.

"Oh, they'll manage," he said. Tears sprung to his eyes. Maybe he would never be invulnerable. "Nancy's a good mother, she'll take care of them. I'll still see them, of course."

I listened to Norman with misty eyes of my own. It happens sometimes. Just when you think you're in control, safely at a distance, you're bushwhacked.

I rolled a cigarette while Norman talked about his decision. I heard him, but part of me was immersed in my own pain. This was close to the bone. I recalled the fateful night I left my wife and three children. The youngest was six. I went to the bus terminal and took the first one that came along. I cried all through the night to Syracuse. And all the way back. That's when I took the basement apartment and plastered my soul on the walls.

"Have you told Nancy?" I asked.

"Yes. She cried." Norman struggled with himself. "She's not happy about it. . . . Well, damn it, neither am I, but it's either leave or shoot myself."

Is he really likely to do that? I wondered. Certainly something in him had to die, but suicide would not be a happy solution.

At the door Norman fumbled in his briefcase. "I meant to show you this. I did it yesterday."

The drawing Norman left was painful to look at, but reassuring. He was juggling a ball. I recalled the dream that took me into analysis—the bouncing ball that kept getting away from me. The gun in the previous drawing was directed at his wife; now it was pointed at himself. A snake was emerging from his mouth, attacking the gun.

The snake in general is a symbol for the unconscious. Its meaning is always ambiguous and specific to the context. Here I saw it as helpful, an inner urge to live; it came out of him, into the world, to meet the threat.

Norman will survive, I thought. He, or something in him, will bite the bullet.

I went back to the drawing of Norman and his wife joined together. Now I saw something I'd missed: between them was an erect penis, aimed directly at their joined hips, their symbiotic connection. To my eyes it was a surge of phallic energy, chthonic masculinity, boring up from below. It was just what was needed if Norman were ever to get quit of the mother.

I put away his file and slept easy.

*

Norman did leave Nancy. A month later he moved out.

As we expected, the separation was not easy. The decision was one thing; he'd worked up to it and felt it to be necessary; carrying it out, making it real, was a new hurdle. Norman saw me twice that week, in agony—not about the break with his wife, which he could live with, but about leaving his kids.

"How is it possible to describe what a father feels when he leaves his children?" I asked Rachel. "How do you convey the grief?" I couldn't help it, I was choked up.

"We have no paradigm for that," I said. "Demeter roams the earth, searching for her daughter Persephone. Inanna mourns the loss of her consort Dumuzi. Isis almost loses her mind looking for the remains of Osiris. In mythology the seasons are suspended in sympathy for women who have lost their loved ones. Are men deemed to be made of sterner stuff? I don't know any myths where a father grieves over his lost children. In fact Saturn eats them."

Rachel mused. I blew my nose and paced the room. Impatience is symptomatic of puer psychology. I knew that, but what can you do.

"It's his anima," she said finally. "She's still close to the mother, so he misses them as a woman would."

I was not satisfied. "Perhaps it's his inner child longing for security. Maybe he's identified with his kids and their needs."

"All that and more," agreed Rachel.

"But how to describe the pain? The guilt?" I wrung my hands and cast about like a demented person.

"Stop that!" said Rachel firmly. "You're getting maudlin."

She who must be obeyed. I stopped pacing and waited.

"I think it's not possible," said Rachel. "Well, not without breaking your temenos. Try the general theme of loneliness."

Yes, of course. In order to consolidate his gains, Norman had to come to terms with loneliness. This I could talk about with some authority. Being without his children was for Norman "merely" a subset of the pervasive loneliness.

Being alone is relatively easy for introverts. They may lack a vital connection with the outer world but they generally have an active inner life. Introverts, unless their extraverted shadow gets constellated, are seldom lonely. Extraverts are used to hustle and bustle; that is their natural milieu, they actively seek it out. Norman, as a card-carrying extrovert, had to learn to live with himself.

Until he made the break, Norman had no personal center. It was projected into his family, a self-contained unit he experienced as wholeness. Without it he felt shattered. Leaving his family created an awesome schism between heaven and earth, the primordial parents. That is the archetypal motif behind the reactions of a child whose parents split up, and Norman, or his inner child, experienced it the same way.

"It's sheer hell," he told me. He'd been out buying furniture, bedding, groceries, making all the decisions himself. "I didn't bargain for this. The tension is driving me crazy."

Norman had never lived alone as a grown man. He'd been in a university residence for two years and shared an apartment with some buddies for another two. In effect, he went from the parental home to a house in the suburbs with his wife, a woman he fell in love with but did not know.

I was thankful Norman wasn't leaving Nancy to live with another woman. If that were the case, he might easily repeat the cycle. Many people do. He needed time alone, time to discover the potential companions in himself. Fortunately he had some tools: his dreams and drawings, personifying his moods, active imagination.

Loneliness feels like one has been abandoned. Collectively, abandonment is associated with the childhood experience of gods and divine heroes—Zeus, Dionysus, Poseidon, Moses, Romulus and Remus, etc. The motif is so widespread in mythology that Jung describes abandonment as "a necessary condition and not just a concomitant symptom," of the potentially higher consciousness symbolized by the child.[7]

A man in the process of becoming independent must detach from his origins: mother, family, society. The same is true for a woman. Sometimes this transition happens smoothly (or appears to). If it does not, the result is two-fold: the "poor me" syndrome, characteristic of the regressive longing for dependence, and a psychic experience of a potentially creative nature (the positive side of the divine child, or puer, archetype): new life, exciting new possibilities.

---

[7] "The Psychology of the Child Archetype," *The Archetypes and the Collective Unconscious,* CW 9i, par. 287.

The incompatibility between these two directions generates a conflict that is invariably present in a midlife crisis. The conflict is the price that has to be paid in order to grow up. It is the cause of the tension Norman has to hold: on the one hand, he longs to return to the past; on the other, he is drawn inexorably toward his unknown future. It's like my dream image of the spider on skis, on a razor blade—riding the edge.

Initially, the conflict goes hand in hand with the feeling of loneliness, behind which is the archetypal motif of the abandoned child. Thus Jung observes,

> Higher consciousness, or knowledge going beyond our present-day consciousness, is equivalent to being *all alone in the world*. This loneliness expresses the conflict between the bearer or symbol of higher consciousness and his surroundings.[8]

Norman continued to see me as he adjusted to his new life, but it was clear that our time together was coming to a close. As he continued to work on himself, he got stronger in every way.

He did not need me as he used to.

*

The particular circumstances that bring a person to a midlife crisis are as multitudinous as grains of sand on a beach. They could not be called unique, however, any more than one grain of sand differs from another.

True, they are always related to the person's individual psychology and life situation. But behind the particularities there are general patterns of thought and behavior that have been universally experienced, and expressed, since the beginning of mankind.

An understanding of these patterns, or archetypes as Jung called them, gives one a perspective on mundane reality. A knowledge of archetypes and archetypal patterns is a kind of blueprint which can be

---

[8] Ibid., par. 288.

overlaid on an individual situation. It is an indispensable tool for Jungian analysts. Norman, as we have seen, was caught up in several of these patterns.

Knowledge is one thing, but true healing does not happen in the head; it occurs through experiential realizations based on feeling. Jung writes:

> Feeling always binds one to the reality and meaning of symbolic contents, and these in turn impose binding standards of ethical behaviour from which aestheticism and intellectualism are only too ready to emancipate themselves.[9]

That is why the analytic process, when pursued on an intellectual level—and that includes most self-analysis—is sterile:

> As long as an analysis moves on the mental plane nothing happens, you can discuss whatever you please, it makes no difference, but when you strike against something below the surface, then a thought comes up in the form of an experience, and stands before you like an object . . . . Whenever you experience a thing that way, you know instantly that it is a fact.[10]

Such "thoughts in the form of an experience" have a transforming effect because they are numinous, overwhelming. They lead to a more balanced perspective: one is merely human—not entirely good (positive inflation), not entirely bad (negative inflation), but a homogenous amalgam of good and evil. The realization and acceptance of this is a mark of the integrated personality.

The process of assimilating unconscious contents does not happen without work. It requires discipline and concentrated application— and a mind receptive to the numinous. Like my attention to the meaning, for me, of elephants. I could have kicked the first one aside. And Norman, he might have said that talking to himself, or playing with colored pencils, was just plain crazy.

---

[9] "The Psychology of the Transference," *The Practice of Psychotherapy*, CW 16, par. 489.

[10] Jung, *The Visions Seminars* (Zurich: Spring Publications, 1976), pp. 337-338.

Jung did not present a systematic therapeutic technique, but he did describe four characteristic stages of the analytic process: confession, elucidation, education and transformation.

In the first stage, you get things off your chest; in the second, you become aware of unconscious contents; in the third, you learn about yourself as a social being; and in the fourth, you change—you become more what you were always meant to be. That is more or less the progression of what Jung called the process of individuation.[11]

"Only what is really oneself," writes Jung, "has the power to heal."[12]

If I were asked to choose one remark of Jung's that informs my attitude as an analyst, that would be it. The whole process is there. Norman is not the first one I've watched it unfold in; he's only the one I felt moved to write about.

What is really oneself can only be discovered through holding the tension between the opposites until a third—the *tertium non datur,* the third not logically given, the unexpected—manifests. This "third," the transcendent function, does not always make itself known in a dramatic way; nor does it necessarily lead to a physical separation from one's mate, as it did with Norman. That depends on individual circumstances.

But it always represents the creative intervention and guidance of the Self, the archetype of wholeness, which in Jung's model of the psyche functions as the regulating center of the personality.

Change is possible. It takes time and effort, and it involves some sacrifice, but it can happen.

---

11 See Marie-Louise von Franz, *C.G. Jung: His Myth in Our Time* (London: Hodder and Stoughton, 1975), pp. 66ff.
12 *Two Essays,* CW 7, par. 258.

9

The End of the Beginning

When you are integrated you are perhaps as unconscious as you ever were, only you no longer project yourself. That is the difference. The aim of the individuation process is not perfection but completeness, and even that is well beyond the reach of most mortals.

—C.G. Jung, *Letters.*

Analysis should release an experience that grips us or falls upon us from above, an experience that has substance and body such as those things which occurred to the ancients. If I were going to symbolize it I would choose the Annunciation.

—C.G. Jung, *Seminar, 1925.*

I said good-bye to Norman with mixed feelings. He arrived in a jaunty mood, wearing a gaudy red tie and a blue blazer.

It was our anniversary. Two years ago he turned up crying in my office. My secretary gave him tea and he spilled it on his pants.

"I celebrated last night," he said. "I went to the opera. I saw *La Bohème* for the first time. God, it was all there!"

"It was?" I asked.

"It's about a sick anima," said Norman. "I've always been a sucker for the frail beauties. Puccini takes it to the extreme." He gestured vaguely. "I see what I was into."

Norman's separation from Nancy was now official. He was leaving analysis not because he thought he didn't need it, but because he had other plans. Life called. Psychologically, he was in pretty good shape; which is to say, he knew what he still had to work on.

He was seeing a woman but he wasn't thinking of marriage.

"We have something special, but I'm happy living on my own," he said airily, as if it were nothing. "She loves me and can show it.

145

And I can feel it." He grinned from ear to ear. "I'm a simple country boy. That's all I ever wanted."

I smiled. "You've come a long way Charlie Brown."

I did not begrudge my appreciation now because Norman had earned it. In the past year we'd been through almost as much as the first. He survived the break with his wife because he took his plight seriously and he worked on himself. You can't ask for more than that. Well, I don't.

Norman was formless when I first saw him—a puddle of water, a bowl of jelly. Now he had some substance. You could see it in his body—the way he held his head, the way he walked, the way his hands moved. And in his eyes.

There was an air of quiet dignity about him. He accepted himself. I respected that.

Norman had brought a dream with him.

"A woman approaches me with a child. It's a boy, a year old, maybe a bit more. The woman is vaguely familiar. She asks me for religious instruction. I tell her she's made a mistake, I'm not a priest. She smiles and hands me the child. I woke up quite mystified."

"What do you make of it?" I asked.

"I suppose the woman is an aspect of my anima, one I don't know very well."

I nodded. "And the child is new life, new possibilities."

"Hey," said Norman,""it's just over a year ago that I left Nancy. That would have been the birth of something new, wouldn't it—the child?"

I agreed. "It would put the conception back in the early months of analysis."

Such dreams are not uncommon. The unconscious is surprising. It often seems to be outside of time and space as we know it. But at times it throws up images that fit in quite well with the sequence of events in everyday life. That is the reality of the psyche.

"What about the religious angle," I said.

Norman shrugged. "It's a mystery to me. You know I don't go to church."

I went to my bookshelf and took out Jung's volume, *Psychology and Religion*. I leafed through it as I spoke. "Jung believed that a neurosis in midlife is never cured without the development of a religious attitude."

"I'm an atheist," said Norman firmly.

"Are you?"

I found the passage I wanted. "Listen to this: 'The term "religion" designates the attitude peculiar to a consciousness which has been changed by experience of the *numinosum*.' "[1]

I flipped pages. "And here Jung says that a man in a conflict situation has to rely on 'divine comfort and mediation . . . . an autonomous psychic happening, a hush that follows the storm, a reconciling light in the darkness . . . secretly bringing order into the chaos of his soul.' "[2]

Norman became pensive.

"That's very interesting," he said finally, "I never thought of it that way."

At the door we embraced. I'd grown attached to Norman.

"Look after the child," I said, "and write if you get work."

We shook hands and I helped him on with his coat. Spring had come, but it was still a bit chilly. The snow hadn't completely melted, but here and there some buds had surfaced. Yesterday Arnold told me it was time to spray the plants.

"Tell me," I said, "did I influence you?" I blushed.

Norman halted in his tracks. He turned to me, astonished. "Of course. My direction was clear but how I got here was not. I would still be nothing without you."

I demurred.

"And have I made a difference to you?" said Norman.

"Yes," I admitted. "At times I was breathless."

Norman beamed. "No kidding."

---

1 "Psychology and Religion," *Psychology and Religion,* CW 11, par. 9.
2 "A Psychological Approach to the Dogma of the Trinity," ibid., par. 260.

*

It was my last appointment for the day. In the past two years I had cut my practice to the bone. Now I often had whole days to myself, completely free. In the winter I played squash. On hot summer days I lay beside the pool, watching the elephant-clouds.

I wandered down to the basement and browsed through the stacks, looking at the pictures. It was very satisfying. I thought about the difference Norman had made to me.

Well, I wasn't bored any more.

But that's another book.

Epilogue

I washed up and put the dishes away. I don't like to leave a messy kitchen when I go to bed.

"What do you think?" I asked.

Rachel had just finished the last chapter.

"I want more," she said. "You can't leave it like this. What started like a textbook became more like a novel. I'm interested in these people. I want to know what became of Norman. And Nancy, you left her in limbo." She paused. "Not to mention Arnold."

I love Rachel, but sometimes she misses the point.

"There's more to say," I acknowledged. "But if I go on from here it becomes too specific. Norman would lose his value as a paradigm of the process."

"If that's true," said Rachel, "then you blew it long ago. After the introduction, everything you talk about is in the context of Norman and Nancy. It also becomes increasingly difficult to tell the difference between you and Norman. You went on to become an analyst. Does Norman?"

"Norman's a businessman. He's quite happy as he is."

"If you are, or were, Norman," she pressed, "then he must become an analyst."

"Look," I said, "I made it all up. There is no Norman, there is no Nancy. They're models for what might take place between two people who get married and start a family. After a few years one of them has a midlife crisis and goes into analysis. The psychology is real, the rest is fiction. I chose to follow the husband because he reminded me of myself, but it might just as well have been the other way around—I could have gone with the wife."

"Tell it to the judge," said Rachel.

I smiled. "Do you know the Grimm fairy tale, 'The Sea-Hare?' "

Rachel shook her head and frowned. She doesn't like being sidetracked.

149

"Too bad for you," I said, and turned out the light.
I don't have to tell her everything.

The author is indebted to everyone he has ever been involved with,
and especially those he has been close to, for the
material that appears in this book.
The characters in it, however, are his own.

Index

abandonment, 140-141
abreaction, 35
active imagination, 131-134, 136,
    140, 142
adaptation, 9, 13, 23-29, 34-36
adolescents, 13, 17
Aeneas, 91
affect, 26, 59
aggression, 81-82
alchemy, 49, 133
analysis: 13-14, 24-25, 34-36, 47-49,
    51-52, 57-58, 60, 80-81, 106,
    109-110, 129, 132, 141-142,
    145-147
    four stages, 143
anima: 27, 29, 59, 63-65, 69-70,
    72-76, 133, 139, 145-146
    as archetype of life, 63
    as muse, 65, 104, 123-126, 149
    -possessed, 64
    as soul, 63, 69-70, 72
    split, 63
    stages of, 64-65
animals, helpful, 90, 105
animus: 27, 29, 71-76, 81, 123-124
    -possessed, 72
    as puer, 86
    stages of, 72-73
Annunciation, 67, 145
anxiety, 9, 13, 16, 29, 34, 40
apathy, 20
Apollo, 89
archetype, archetypal image/motif,
    14, 21, 29, 39, 55, 57-59,
    90-92, 124, 140-143

Arnold, 48, 68, 70, 93, 99-104, 106,
    137, 147, 149
astrology, 118
Attis, 108

ball, 52, 58-59, 138
Beckett, Samuel, 116
Bes, 129
Boa, Fraser, 57n
Boris, 33, 84, 106, 113, 119-120
Buddha, 67
burning house, in dream, 47, 59

Cabiri, 129
Campbell, Joseph, 91n
causal view, of neurosis, 18-21
change, 37, 143
chaos, 31, 35, 147
child, 140-141, 146-147
Christ, 90
chthonic wisdom, 129
commitment, 41, 50, 87, 106, 109
compassion, 51, 120
compensation, 17, 27, 29, 53-55, 59,
    65, 70, 80, 82, 116
complex(es) (*see also* father complex,
    mother complex, Oedipus
    complex): 16, 21, 29, 38-41, 50,
    58-59, 66, 68, 74-76, 81, 98, 116
    objectifying, 75
    depotentiating, 38, 55
    in dreams, 55, 59
    indicators, 39
    personified, 38, 40, 55, 132-133
confession, 143

conflict: 9, 13-14, 16, 18, 22-23, 28-29, 35-38, 44, 48, 53-54, 71, 79, 141, 147
   and dreams, 53-54, 59
   Oedipal, 18
   between shadow and persona, 41-43, 82-84
   and tension, 18, 23, 26, 29, 36-38, 49
confusion, 29, 32, 35, 98, 133
container, as temenos, 48-49, 59, 75, 132
container/contained, in relationship, 74
countertransference, 76
crippledom, 129
crucifixion, 90, 116
Cybele, 108

Dante, 65, 90
dark night of the soul, 91
Daumal, René, 108, 125
deflation, 39, 103
Demeter, 139
depression, 9, 13, 16, 20, 25, 29, 34, 47, 62-64, 85, 92, 98, 110, 127, 132-134
diagnosis, 12-13
differentiation, 40, 81, 87, 116
Dionysus, 86, 89, 140
dismemberment, 90, 116
dissociation, 12, 16-17, 26
Don Juan, 44, 64, 70, 123, 135
Dr. Jekyll and Mr. Hyde, 80
dream(s): 40, 49, 51-59, 128, 140
   archetypal, 55, 58-59
   of ball, 52, 58-59
   of burning house, 47, 108
   of child, 146
   and compensation, 53-55, 80
   control of, 56

   of desert, 105
   of dismemberment, 116
   dramatic structure, 56
   of dwarfs, 105
   Freud's view, 53, 57
   of giant, 115
   of horse, 78
   initial, 51-52, 108
   of Jung, 110
   as mirror, 53
   of mother, 47, 107-108
   objective/subjective levels, 58, 79
   of phallus, 72
   of prince and princess, 135-136
   purpose of, 52-54
   of spider on skis, 54, 141
Dumuzi, 139
dwarfs, 105, 129

Einstein, Albert, 94
élan vital, 19
elephant, 66-67, 70, 142, 148
emotion (*see also* affect), 34, 40, 75, 98
empathy, 26, 44, 68, 71, 90
energic view, of psyche, 19-23
energy (*see also* libido): conservation of, 19-21, 25
   flow of, 19-29, 34, 43-44, 52
equivalence, principle of, 20, 22
Eros, 86, 108
experiential realizations, 142
extraversion, 27-28, 95, 98, 100, 137, 139
eyes, 108, 110, 146

fairy tales, 57, 90, 105, 108, 124, 133
faithless Eros, 108
falling in love, 63, 66, 70, 76, 140
fantasies, 18-19, 23-24, 34-35, 79, 82, 87, 124, 135

father: archetype, 124
  complex, 37, 72, 124
Faust, 15
fear, 13, 29, 40, 128
feeling function, 17, 26-27, 34, 37,
  75, 94-98, 105, 142
feeling-toned ideas, 39
fetish, 66
final view, of neurosis, 19-23
fisher king, 129
fixation, Oedipal, 18-19, 21
free association, 57
Freud, 18-20, 24-26, 40, 53, 55, 79

giant, 115-116
Gilgamesh, 90
glass mountain, 108
Goethe, 15
Goliath, 124, 134
good, as enemy of better, 85
Grail Legend, 129
grief, 139
guilt, 13, 29, 34, 40, 43, 49, 107,
  110, 120, 139

Harpocrates, 129
helpful animals, 90, 105
Hephaestus, 129
Hermes, 73
hero, 90-92, 108, 116, 123-124, 129
Hero with a Thousand Faces, 91n
homosexuality, 135
hook, for projections, 69, 108, 124
horse, 78-80

I Ching, 31, 88-89
Iacchus, 86
identification: 48, 68-71, 124, 139
  with mother, 50
  with persona, 43

impatience, 106, 139
impotence, 64, 77, 79, 125, 136
imprisonment, 88-90
Inanna, 139
incest, 19, 51, 125
individuation: 11, 14-15, 29, 70-71,
  110, 143, 145
  definition, 11
  and emotion, 75
  refusal of, 88
infancy, 18, 24
infantile fantasies, 18-19, 29, 34-35, 82
inferior function, 17, 27, 29, 96-97
Inferno, 65
inflation: 35, 47, 108, 134, 142
  negative, 110, 128, 142
insecurity, 85
intellectualism, 142
introversion, 28, 95, 98, 100, 139
intuition, 84, 95-104, 111, 118
Isis, 129, 139

jealousy, 33, 120
Jonah, 91
Jung, C.G., 9, 11-28, 37-41, 52-55,
  57, 61, 66, 68, 75, 81-82, 91,
  93-96, 98, 110, 115, 127, 140-
  143, 145-147

Kafka, Franz, 45, 77, 88, 127-128, 134
Kierkegaard, Soren, 105, 125
knot, in stomach, 33, 35, 44, 62, 127
Kundalini yoga, 67

La Bohème, 145
Lawrence, D.H., 79
libido: 19-28
  progression of, 25-26
  regression of, 26-28
limitations, 16, 19, 88-89

loneliness, 139-141
loss of soul, 63-64, 69-70

Mani, 129
marijuana, 33, 46, 50, 77, 105, 114,
    117-118, 134
"Marriage as a Psychological
    Relationship," 74
Maya, Queen, 67
mechanistic view, of psyche, 18-20
medical model, 16
Midas, King, 40
midlife crisis: and dreams, 52, 55-59
    and neurosis, 9, 11-29, 147
    and persona, 41-44
    physical symptoms, 24, 36-37
    and puer psychology, 86-90
    purpose of, 16-19
    and shadow, 82-85
    and typology, 96-97
Miro, Joan, 34
moods: 13, 25, 29, 39, 64, 68, 117
    personifying, 132-133, 140
Moses, 140
mother: archetype, 21, 39
    complex, 39-40, 44, 50, 59, 61, 70-
        71, 80, 85, 89-90, 92, 104, 106-
        108, 114-116, 123, 133, 135-138
    identification with, 50
mountain, 108, 133, 135
mountain-anima, 133
muladhara chakra, 67
Myers-Briggs Type Indicator, 94
myths/mythology, 57, 73, 80, 86,
    89-92, 108, 129, 139-140

Nancy, 33-34, 43-46, 49-51, 61-63,
    65, 69, 71-74, 77-79, 98, 106,
    111- 114, 116-120, 123-128,
    130, 135-138, 145, 149

negative inflation, 110, 128
nervous breakdown, 11, 18, 96-97
neurosis: 9, 11-29, 40
    acute, 9, 12-13
    and adaptation, 23-28
    as attempt at self-cure, 17, 25-29
    and conflict, 37
    definition, 11, 16-17, 24
    energic viewpoint, 19-23
    final view, 19-23
    mechanistic view, 18-20
    and medical model, 16
    physical symptoms, 24, 36-37
    and puer psychology, 86-90
    purpose of, 9, 16-19, 54
    reductive view, 18, 20
    symptoms, 9, 13, 16-17, 20-21, 24,
        26, 29, 34, 36-37
    synthetic view, 18
Nietzsche, Friedrich, 115, 125
night sea journey, 90-92
nigredo, 133
Notebooks of Malte Laurids Brigge, 114
numinosity, 29, 52, 142, 147

Odysseus, 91
Oedipus complex, 18-19, 24, 38
one-sidedness, 17, 25, 37, 54, 104
opinion(s), 35, 45, 51, 72, 81
opposites, 17-18, 22-23, 26-29, 36, 38,
    89, 105, 116, 143
Osiris, 129, 139

participation mystique, 48-49
penises, clay, 134
perfection, 14, 82, 145
Persephone, 139
persona: 27, 41-43, 70
    regressive restoration of, 128-129
    and shadow, 82-84, 134-135

personality, disintegration of, 11-12
Peter Pan, 86
phoenix, 92
Picture of Dorian Gray, The, 86
Pinocchio, 91
"poor me" syndrome, 134, 140
Poseidon, 140
possibilities, 77, 89, 96, 102-103,
    111, 128, 140, 146
prison, 88-89
progression, of energy, 25-29, 34
projection(s): 36, 57-58, 63, 66-73,
    76, 82, 97, 124-125, 137, 145
    withdrawal of, 69, 71
provisional life, 87-88
psyche: reality of, 53-54, 146
    self-regulation of, 9, 17-29,
    52-54, 59
Psychological Types, 94, 96
Psychology and Religion, 147
psychoneurosis, 13, 16
Puccini, 145
puella, 86
puer aeternus, 86, 89
puer psychology, 86-90, 105, 124,
    139-140

Rachel, 104, 123-126, 130, 132, 139,
    149-150
rake-hell, 44, 61
raven, 133-134, 136
reductive view, of neurosis, 18, 20
regression, of energy, 21, 23-24,
    26-29, 34, 40, 126-127, 140
relationship(s), 53-54, 58, 64, 68-76,
    80, 82, 94-104, 106, 109
religion, 57, 90-91, 146-147
repression, 23, 26-27, 44, 53, 81
Rilke, Rainer Maria, 42-43, 114
Rocking-Horse Winner, The, 79

sacrifice, 87, 143
Saturn, 89, 139
scapegoating, 82
"Sea-Hare, The," 149
Secret Life of Walter Mitty, The, 81
secrets, 48-49
Self, 29, 143
self-analysis, 142
self-containment, *see* container
self-examination, 15, 94
self-knowledge, 53, 82
self-pity, 34, 40, 79, 130
self-regulation of psyche, 9, 17-29,
    52-54, 59
self-righteousness, 79
senex, 89, 124
sensation function, 84, 95-104, 111
sentimentality, 64, 68
shadow: 23, 27, 29, 44, 70, 79-87,
    92, 106, 111, 116, 139
    assimilation of, 84, 97-104, 135
    and persona, 82-84, 134-135
    positive aspects, 85-86
    of puer, 89
silence, 106
sleeplessness, 13, 34
snake, 67, 112, 138
son-lover, 50-51, 136
Sophia, 64-65, 73
soul, 15, 63-65, 69-70, 72, 82, 88,
    91, 110, 132, 137, 147
spider on skis, 54, 141
spontaneity, 87, 90
stealing, 82-83
suggestion, 28, 68
suicide, 13, 34, 40, 138
superior function, 96-97, 129
symbiosis, 34, 138
symbol(s): 21-22, 29, 118
    in dreams, 53-60

symptoms: 9, 13, 16-17, 20-21, 24, 26, 29, 34, 40
   physical, 24, 36-37
synchronicity, 29, 66, 125
synthetic view, of neurosis, 18

Tao, 14
temenos (*see also* container), 49, 51, 58, 75, 134, 139
Ten Thousand Dreams Interpreted, 56
tension, 18, 23, 26, 29, 36-37, 48-49, 105, 140-141, 143
Terrible Mother, 107, 115
tertium non datur, 143
Theseus, 40
thinking function, 17, 27, 34, 84, 95-98
togetherness, 70-71
transcendent function, 29, 38, 143
transference, 76, 93, 135
transformation, 14, 22, 142-143
typology, 27, 84, 93-104

unconscious: connection with consciousness, 14, 17, 24, 36, 53-56, 70-71, 73, 116, 131-134, 142
   contents, 26-29, 35, 47, 53, 77, 81, 142-143
   as mother, 92
unlived life, 85

vas Hermetis, 49
von Franz, Marie-Louise, 57n, 77, 89

Way of the Dream, The, 57n
whale-dragon, 92
wholeness: 14-15, 29, 140
   archetype of, 143
wife as horse, in dream, 79-80
will power, 23, 53
Wisdom (Sophia), 64-65, 73
wise old man, 65, 76
Word Association Experiment, 39

Zeus, 140

Studies in Jungian Psychology
by Jungian Analysts

Limited Edition Paperbacks

Prices and payment in U.S. dollars (except for Canadian orders)

1. The Secret Raven: Conflict and Transformation.
Daryl Sharp (Toronto). ISBN 0-919123-00-7. 128 pp. $13
A practical study of *puer* psychology, including dream interpretation and material on midlife crisis, the provisional life, the mother complex, anima and shadow. Illustrated.

2. The Psychological Meaning of Redemption Motifs in Fairytales.
Marie-Louise von Franz (Zurich). ISBN 0-919123-01-5. 128 pp. $13
Unique approach to understanding typical dream motifs (bathing, clothes, animals, etc.).

3. On Divination and Synchronicity: The Psychology of Meaningful Chance.
Marie-Louise von Franz (Zurich). ISBN 0-919123-02-3. 128 pp. $13
Penetrating study of irrational methods of divining fate (I Ching, astrology, palmistry, Tarot cards, etc.), contrasting Western ideas with those of so-called primitives. Illustrated.

4. The Owl Was a Baker's Daughter: Obesity, Anorexia and the Repressed Feminine.
Marion Woodman (Toronto). ISBN 0-919123-03-1. 144 pp. $14
A modern classic, with particular attention to the body as mirror of the psyche in weight disturbances and eating disorders. Based on case studies, dreams and mythology. Illus.

5. Alchemy: An Introduction to the Symbolism and the Psychology.
Marie-Louise von Franz (Zurich). ISBN 0-919123-04-X. 288 pp. $18
Detailed guide to what the alchemists were really looking for: emotional wholeness. Invaluable for interpreting images and motifs in modern dreams and drawings. **84 illustrations.**

6. Descent to the Goddess: A Way of Initiation for Women.
Sylvia Brinton Perera (New York). ISBN 0-919123-05-8. 112 pp. $12
A timely and provocative study of the need for an inner, female authority in a masculine-oriented society. Rich in insights from mythology and the author's analytic practice.

7. The Psyche as Sacrament: C.G. Jung and Paul Tillich.
John P. Dourley (Ottawa). ISBN 0-919123-06-6. 128 pp. $13
Comparative study from a dual perspective (author is Catholic priest and Jungian analyst), exploring the psychological meaning of religion, God, Christ, the spirit, the Trinity, etc.

8. Border Crossings: Carlos Castaneda's Path of Knowledge.
Donald Lee Williams (Boulder). ISBN 0-919123-07-4. 160 pp. $14
The first thorough psychological examination of the Don Juan novels, bringing Castaneda's spiritual journey down to earth. Special attention to the psychology of the feminine.

9. Narcissism and Character Transformation. The Psychology of Narcissistic Character Disorders.
ISBN 0-919123-08-2. 192 pp. $15
Nathan Schwartz-Salant (New York).
A comprehensive study of narcissistic character disorders, drawing upon a variety of analytic points of view (Jung, Freud, Kohut, Klein, etc.). Theory and clinical material. Illus.

10. Rape and Ritual: A Psychological Study.
Bradley A. Te Paske (Minneapolis). ISBN 0-919123-09-0. 160 pp. $14
Incisive combination of theory, clinical material and mythology. Illustrated.

11. Alcoholism and Women: The Background and the Psychology.
Jan Bauer (Montreal). ISBN 0-919123-10-4. 144 pp. $14
Sociology, case material, dream analysis and archetypal patterns from mythology.

12. Addiction to Perfection: The Still Unravished Bride.
Marion Woodman (Toronto). ISBN 0-919123-11-2. 208 pp. $15
A powerful and authoritative look at the psychology of modern women. Examines dreams, mythology, food rituals, body imagery, sexuality and creativity. A continuing best-seller since its original publication in 1982. Illustrated.

13. Jungian Dream Interpretation: A Handbook of Theory and Practice.
James A. Hall, M.D. (Dallas). ISBN 0-919123-12-0. 128 pp. $13
A practical guide, including common dream motifs and many clinical examples.

14. The Creation of Consciousness: Jung's Myth for Modern Man.
Edward F. Edinger, M.D. (Los Angeles). ISBN 0-919123-13-9. 128 pp. $13
Insightful study of the meaning and purpose of human life. Illustrated.

15. The Analytic Encounter: Transference and Human Relationship.
Mario Jacoby (Zurich). ISBN 0-919123-14-7. 128 pp. $13
Sensitive exploration of the difference between relationships based on projection and
I-Thou relationships characterized by mutual respect and psychological objectivity.

16. Change of Life: Psychological Study of Dreams and the Menopause.
Ann Mankowitz (Santa Fe). ISBN 0-919123-15-5. 128 pp. $13
A moving account of an older woman's Jungian analysis, dramatically revealing the later
years as a time of rebirth, a unique opportunity for psychological development.

17. The Illness That We Are: A Jungian Critique of Christianity.
John P. Dourley (Ottawa). ISBN 0-919123-16-3. 128 pp. $13
Radical study by Catholic priest and analyst, exploring Jung's qualified appreciation of
Christian symbols and ritual, while questioning the masculine ideals of Christianity.

18. Hags and Heroes: A Feminist Approach to Jungian Therapy with Couples.
Polly Young-Eisendrath (Philadelphia). ISBN 0-919123-17-1. 192 pp. $15
Highly original integration of feminist views with the concepts of Jung and Harry Stack
Sullivan. Detailed strategies and techniques, emphasis on feminine authority.

19. Cultural Attitudes in Psychological Perspective.
Joseph Henderson , M.D. (San Francisco). ISBN 0-919123-18-X. 128 pp. $13
Shows how a psychological attitude can give depth to one's world view. Illustrated.

20. The Vertical Labyrinth: Individuation in Jungian Psychology.
Aldo Carotenuto (Rome). ISBN 0-919123-19-8. 144 pp. $14
A guided journey through the world of dreams and psychic reality, illustrating the process
of individual psychological development.

21. The Pregnant Virgin: A Process of Psychological Transformation.
Marion Woodman (Toronto). ISBN 0-919123-20-1. 208 pp. $16
A celebration of the feminine, in both men and women. Explores the wisdom of the body,
eating disorders, relationships, dreams, addictions, etc. Illustrated.

22. Encounter with the Self: William Blake's *Illustrations of the Book of Job.*
Edward F. Edinger, M.D. (Los Angeles). ISBN 0-919123-21-X. 80 pp. $10
Penetrating commentary on the Biblical Job story as a numinous, archetypal event.
Complete with Blake's original 22 engravings.

23. The Scapegoat Complex: Toward a Mythology of Shadow and Guilt.
Sylvia Brinton Perera (New York). ISBN 0-919123-22-8. 128 pp. $13
A hard-hitting study of victim psychology in modern men and women, based on case
material, mythology and archetypal patterns.

24. The Bible and the Psyche: Individuation Symbolism in the Old Testament.
Edward F. Edinger (Los Angeles). ISBN 0-919123-23-6. 176 pp. $15
A major new work relating significant Biblical events to the psychological movement
toward wholeness that takes place in individuals.

25. The Spiral Way: A Woman's Healing Journey.
Aldo Carotenuto (Rome). ISBN 0-919123-24-4. 144 pp. $14
Detailed case history of a fifty-year-old woman's Jungian analysis, with particular attention
to her dreams and the rediscovery of her enthusiasm for life.

26. The Jungian Experience: Analysis and Individuation.
James A. Hall, M.D. (Dallas). ISBN 0-919123-25-2. 176 pp. $15
Comprehensive study of the theory and clinical application of Jungian thought, including
Jung's model, the structure of analysis, where to find an analyst, training centers, etc.

27. Phallos: Sacred Image of the Masculine.
Eugene Monick (Scranton/New York). ISBN 0-919123-26-0. 144 pp. $14
Uncovers the essence of masculinity (as opposed to the patriarchy) through close examination of the physical, mythological and psychological aspects of phallos. **30 illustrations.**

28. The Christian Archetype: A Jungian Commentary on the Life of Christ.
Edward F. Edinger, M.D. (Los Angeles). ISBN 0-919123-27-9. 144 pp. $14
Psychological view of images and events central to the Christian myth, showing their symbolic meaning in terms of personal individuation. **31 illustrations.**

29. Love, Celibacy and the Inner Marriage.
John P. Dourley (Ottawa). ISBN 0-919123-28-7. 128 pp. $13
Shows that without a deeply compassionate relationship to the inner anima/animus, we cannot relate to our intimates or to God, to the full depth of our ability to love.

30. Touching: Body Therapy and Depth Psychology.
Deldon Anne McNeely (Lynchburg, VA). ISBN 0-919123-29-5. 128 pp. $13
Illustrates how these two disciplines, both concerned with restoring life to an ailing human psyche, may be integrated in theory and practice. Focus on the healing power of touch.

31. Personality Types: Jung's Model of Typology.
Daryl Sharp (Toronto). ISBN 0-919123-30-9. 128 pp. $13
Detailed explanation of Jung's model (basis for the widely-used Myers-Briggs Type Indicator), showing its implications for individual development and for relationships. Illus.

32. The Sacred Prostitute: Eternal Aspect of the Feminine.
Nancy Qualls-Corbett (Birmingham). ISBN 0-919123-31-7. 176 pp. $15
Shows how our vitality and capacity for joy depend on rediscovering the ancient connection between spirituality and passionate love. Illustrated. **(Foreword by Marion Woodman.)**

33. When the Spirits Come Back.
Janet O. Dallett (Seal Harbor, WA). ISBN 0-919123-32-5. 160 pp. $14
An analyst examines herself, her profession and the limitations of prevailing attitudes toward mental disturbance. Interweaving her own story with descriptions of those who come to her for help, she details her rediscovery of the integrity of the healing process.

34. The Mother: Archetypal Image in Fairy Tales.
Sibylle Birkhäuser-Oeri (Zurich). ISBN 0-919123-33-3. 176 pp. $15
Compares processes in the unconscious with common images and motifs in folk-lore. Illustrates how positive and negative mother complexes affect us all, with examples from many well-known fairy tales and daily life. **(Edited by Marie-Louise von Franz.)**

35. The Survival Papers: Anatomy of a Midlife Crisis.
Daryl Sharp (Toronto). ISBN 0-919123-34-1. 160 pp. $15
Jung's major concepts—persona, shadow, anima and animus, complexes, projection, typology, active imagination, individuation, etc.—are powerfully presented in the immediate context of an analysand's process. And the analyst's. We are there as they both struggle with the conflict between the security of a hard-won, successful lifestyle and an inner imperative that demands a total reassessment of self—with no guarantees. Illustrated.

36. The Cassandra Complex: Living with Disbelief.
Laurie Layton Schapira (New York). ISBN 0-919123-35-X. 160 pp. $15
A close look at how hysteria manifests in the female psyche, and why it threatens patriarchal values. Includes clinical material and an examination of the role of powerfully intuitive, medial women through history. Shows how unconscious, prophetic sensibilities can be transformed from a burden into a valuable source of conscious understanding. Illustrated.

Prices and payment (check or money order) in U.S. dollars

Please add $1 per book (bookpost) or $3 per book (airmail)

INNER CITY BOOKS
Box 1271, Station Q, Toronto, Canada
M4T 2P4